CONFLICTS OF INTEREST IN THE CHANGING FINANCIAL WORLD

Edited by R. M. Goode

The Institute of Bankers

Centre for Commercial Law Studies
Queen Mary College · University of London

THE INSTITUTE OF BANKERS
10 Lombard Street
London EC3V 9AS

© The Institute of Bankers 1986 and Centre for Commercial Law Studies, Queen Mary College, University of London.

 British Library Cataloguing in Publication Data

1. Conflicts of interest in the changing financial world – Great Britain
I. Stock Exchange   Goode, R. M.
332.64'241   HG5432

ISBN 0 85297 167 2

Typeset in 10/11pt Times Roman
Text printed on 115 gsm Silverwhite Cartridge.
Cover on 115 gsm New Edition Bookjacket
by Butler & Tanner Ltd, Frome and London

CONFLICTS OF INTEREST IN THE CHANGING FINANCIAL WORLD

CONTENTS

TABLE OF STATUTES

TABLE OF CASES

ABBREVIATIONS

CSI Council for the Securities Industry
DTI Department of Trade and Industry
EEC European Economic Community
SEC Securities and Exchange Commission
SIB Securities and Investments Board
SRO Self regulating organisation

THE CONTRIBUTORS

Professor Roy Goode, OBE, LLD – Crowther Professor of Credit and Commercial Law, Director of the Centre for Commercial Law Studies, Queen Mary College, University of London.

Professor Robert R. Pennington, LLD, Professor of Commercial Law, Birmingham University

Professor L. C. B. (Jim) Gower, LLM, Professor Emeritus, Southampton University, Consultant, Securities and Investments Board.

Terence Prime, BA (Law), Solicitor, Lecturer in Law, University of Liverpool.

Michael Fowle, MA, FCA, Partner in charge of the UK banking and finance practice, Peat Marwick Mitchell & Co, Chartered Accountants, and Deputy Chairman of the Peat Marwick International Banking and Finance Group.

Philip Wood, BA (Capetown), BA (Oxon), Partner, Allen & Overy, Solicitors, Visiting Fellow, Kings College, University of London.

Lawrence Collins, MA, LLB (Cantab), LLM (Columbia, New York), Partner, Herbert Smith & Co, Solicitors, Fellow of Wolfson College, Cambridge, Visiting Professor, Queen Mary College, University of London.

INTRODUCTION

The annual seminar held jointly by the Institute of Bankers and the Centre for Commercial Law Studies at Highgate House, Creaton, on a major theme relevant to banking law and practice has become noted not only for the high level of debate but also for the topicality of the subject. This was particularly true of the 1985 seminar, on Conflicts of Interest in the Changing Financial World, which was held just before the introduction of the Financial Services Bill, a legislative measure designed to accommodate the impending revolution in the structure, organisation and management of the securities industry popularly known as the Big Bang. This book consists of the principal papers delivered at the seminar, revised and updated and with tables and an index.

The new regime for the securities industry was conceived and brought to fruition by Professor Jim Gower, who by dint of imagination, persuasion and a dogged regusal to be deflected from his goal, converted the initially hostile City institutions to his way of thinking and brought about almost single-handed the sweeping reforms described in this book – a truly remarkable achievement. The essence of Jim Gower's scheme is self-regulation within a statutory framework. The catalyst for change and the objectives of the new regime are succinctly described in his paper, 'Conflicts of Interest and the City Revolution,' in which he points out that whilst it is necessary to have rules to prevent fraud and other abuse, the primary purpose of the new system of regulation is not to prevent fraud but to give the investing public an assurance of competence on the part of those who undertake investment business.

It is now widely accepted that conflicts of interest are inescapable, owing to the growth of financial conglomerates and the abolition of the Stock Exchange single capacity rule which has hitherto precluded brokers from acting on their own behalf as well as for clients. The most we can expect to achieve is to manage conflicts of interest in such a way that clients are neither prejudiced nor misled. Such management involves a combination of structural, organisational and regulatory devices. Those wishing to engage in investment business can be required to obtain authorisation to do so from an approved body, with a view to ensuring the integrity and competence of practitioners in the market. Conglomerates can be broken up or Chinese walls can be erected between the different parts of an institution acting in different capacities so as to prevent the spread of relevant information from one to the other. Rules can be formulated requiring full disclosure, 'best execution' (i.e. better terms when dealing for a client than when the institution is dealing for its own account) and subordination of the interests of the institution to those of the client. Compliance officers can be appointed within each authorised institution to act as an internal watchdog in securing observance of the letter and spirit of the rules. The Financial Services Bill prohibits any person from carrying on an investment business unless he is authorised or exempt, and provides for rules to be made by the Secretary of State regulating the conduct of investment business. The primary instrument of control is to be the Securities and Investments Board. A person wishing to carry on an investment business may obtain authorisation directly from the Board and submit himself to the SIB rules or he may qualify automatically by virtue of his membership of a recognised self-regulating organisation. It will be the task of the SIB to formulate rules for those to whom it grants direct authorisation and to approve the rules of the SROs and ensure that they are duly performing their functions in regard to the admission, expulsion and disciplining of their members and the monitoring and enforcement of their rules. The rules of the SIB and SROs will embody, among other things, the principles of disclosure, best execution and subordination of interest.

But what constitutes a conflict of interest? Professor Robert Pennington's paper formulates the basic principle in the following terms:

'The underlying principle of equity is that a person who acts as representative of another is in a conflict of interest situation if, either at the time when he accepts appointment or subsequently while he acts as a representative, there is a material interest of his own or of a third person for whom he also acts, and the pursuit or protection of that interest would create a substantial risk that he may not act in the best way to pursue or protect the interest of the person he represents.'

Starting from the premise that conflicts of interest are inevitable, Professor Pennington identifies some typical situations in which a conflict of interest may arise – a topic developed in Philip Wood's paper – and draws attention to the difficulty of reconciling open competition with adequate client protection. In presenting his paper, he emphasized the impracticability of applying a single rule of equity to all types of business and the need to formulate different rules for different types of enterprise.

Terence Prime provides us with a detailed examination of the rules of law and equity that have traditionally governed conflicts of interest, taking the position of the bank as the paradigm. Three situations are to be distinguished. In the first, the person with whom the bank deals is not the bank's customer, and the bank deals with him exclusively in its own interest, as where it takes a guarantee. In the second, the bank deals with a customer but its activity does not involve any agency relationship between itself and the customer – e.g. the bank merely gives investment advice, as opposed to buying and selling investments for the customer. In the third situation, the bank acts as agent for its customer, as where it deals in investments on his behalf. Whilst a conflict may arise between the interests of the bank and the interests of its customer, the more common form of conflict is between the interests of one customer and those of another. The duties imposed in the bank in relation to conflicts of interest may derive either from contract or as a matter of equitable obligation, typically because the circumstances of the relationship between banker and customer are such as to create a fiduciary duty on the part of the bank. The treatment of confidential information raised a particular problem the resolution of which is not always easy. Mr. Prime considers that in *North and South Trust Co. v. Berkeley*[1] the court reached the wrong conclusion.

Conflict of interest situations are not, of course, confined to financial institutions. Members of the professions are also called upon to consider from time to time to whom their duties are primarily owed and how to deal with a conflict of loyalties. Michael Fowle's instructive and thought-provoking paper examines the ways in which members of the accountancy profession seek to tackle such problems. In 1982 the Institute of Chartered Accountants in England and Wales enunciated a set of principles in its *Guide to Professional Ethics*, emphasizing the importance of objectivity, impartiality, integrity and confidentiality. Accounting, as Mr. Fowle points out, is not an exact science; it involves professional judgments on a range of matters on which there is often room for diversity of opinions and approaches. One of the prime responsibilities of accountants is to audit the accounts prepared by management and to see that these provide a true and fair view of the company. The perceptions of the auditor may differ sharply from those of management, but it is not the function of the auditor to impose his own views as to proper accounting treatment; the accounts are those of the management, not of the

1. [1971] 1 All ER 980

auditors, and should be accepted if they embody an approach which is within the range of acceptable choices, even if it is not the approach the auditor himself would adopt. A crucial problem for the auditor is to identify the client. Though management selects the auditor, it is the shareholders who are the clients. On the other hand, the auditor has to work with management; the problem is how to regain the confidence of the Board whilst still doing his job. And if the auditor suspects manipulation or fraud, to whom should he report?

Philip Wood's paper gives a practising solicitor's perception of conflicts of duty and interest in investment banking, tackling a number of highly practical questions. What are the advantages and disadvantages of integration in the provision of financial services? How effective are Chinese walls? What are the circumstances in which a broker may find himself in conflict with a client? What conflict problems may be expected to arise in fund management and the operation of discretionary accounts, in underwriting, in corporate finance and in the management of new issues? In his oral presentation, Philip Wood raised a question as to whether English law was too tough, whether the standard it required of fiduciaries (assuming you could identify a fiduciary) was too exacting. By contrast with French law, which was concerned for the small man, English law was very business orientated, yet it was also moralistic, with a strong emphasis on honesty. The problem was to maintain proper standards of business behaviour without unduly impairing business efficiency.

Two further presentations were made, by Jonathan Lass (then of Citibank) and William Stuttaford (Laurence Prust & Co., stockbrokers). Mr Lass identified four types of player in the new financial market: conglomerates, offering as wide a range of services under one group structure as possible; niche providers, focussing on a narrow range of specialist services, with the emphasis on quality, flexibility and independence; abstainers, who would hold back and hope to learn from the mistakes of their competitors; and special cases, such as the break-up of a conglomerate into independent, specialist units. Particular problems could be expected to arise in the case of the conglomerates. Regulation of some kind was clearly needed, but did the proposed new structure embody the right approach? Mr Lass felt that the SROs might not work too well in practice. The distribution of responsibility among so many SROs produced fragmentation of control, inadequacy of resources and the likelihood of conflicting rules. It would be better to rely exclusively on the SIB, which could recruit professionals with experience of the market place. These fears of fragmentation and conflict of rules were echoed by other speakers, who pointed out that an organisation engaged in investment operations falling within two SROs might find itself faced with the need to comply with requirements which either conflicted or differed in points of detail, thus duplicating the task of compliance.

Bill Stuttaford demonstrated how his own group had decided to deal with the problem by moving away from the conglomerate concept and splitting itself up into separate and independent units, each with its own specific function: research, market-making, fund management, corporate finance and advisory services for private clients. The combination of any two of these activities in one enterprise would or might produce conflicts of interest.

In the final paper reproduced in this volume, on Banking Secrecy and the Enforcement of Securities Legislation, Lawrence Collins discusses some of the problems that may arise where a person resident in a country whose laws require him to maintain confidentiality is required by legislation or court orders in another country to disclose information or produce documents contrary to the prohibition imposed by his own laws. For example, a UK company wishing to exercise its statutory right to ascertain who are the beneficial owners of its shares may seek to obtain information from a bank or other registered owner located in another jurisdiction by the laws of which that owner is bound to secrecy. Conversely, a foreign court may make an order for production of documents or disclosure of information against a British bank compliance with which would breach the bank's duty of confidentiality under English law. Placed between the devil and the deep blue sea, what is the party in question supposed to do? There have been several recent cases of such conflict in which courts have held that the existence of a foreign secrecy law was not necessarily an answer to a charge of contempt of a court order directing disclosure. Ultimately, conflicts of this kind can be resolved only at the political level.

It will be apparent from a reading of the excellent papers contained in this book that the regulation of conflicts of interest in the securities market will be far from easy. Identifying a conflict situation, simple in theory, can be much harder in practice. Those who deal daily in securities do not enjoy the luxury of quiet contemplation ascribed to trustees by courts of equity in the nineteenth century; they frequently have to make quick decisions, for good or ill, in the course of transacting a heavy volume of business, and the individual concerned will not necessarily be aware of information possessed by other parts of his organisation which might suggest a possible conflict of interest. Moreover, the speed and volume of business that can now be accommodated by modern technology may make it difficult to identify any particular transaction as linked to another.

The formulation of detailed rules of conduct, necessary though this may be, is not without dangers. In particular, it may encourage the less well-informed or less scrupulous player to believe that if he conforms to the prescribed rules he cannot be faulted, whereas the truth is that the law does not find it too difficult to recognize cheating or sharp practice, and no amount of compliance with the letter of the rules will by itself give immunity from the legal or equitable consequences of unfair dealing. It is important to introduce into each set of rules, so far as not already provided by the legislation itself, a general requirement of good faith and fair dealing, over and above such specific rules of conduct as may be prescribed.

Finally, there is the whole question of enforcement. Who, ultimately, is to be responsible for policing the securities industry and for ensuring that the rules are enforced. Government departments sponsoring legislation tend to regard their task as done when the statute is enacted, and are usually unwilling to commit resources to its enforcement, still less to a study of its effectiveness. Indeed, in these times of financial constraint departments are likely to find that their budgets are slashed by a hard-nosed Treasury, so that even if willing they lack the resources to police the new law. Hence it is likely that the main burden of securing compliance both with the letter of the new rules and with their spirit will fall on the SIB. It is to be hoped that the Board will take a tough line from the outset – particularly with any major institution that transgresses – in order to establish the required standard and to ensure that the decision to allow a wide measure of self-regulation to the securities industry was justified.

I should like to express my warm thanks to Alan Miller, Under-Secretary, The Institute of Bankers, for all his work in organising the present publication; to Mrs Anne Lyons for preparing the index and Eynon Smart for compiling the tables of statutes and cases and correcting the proofs; and Miss Hilary Norman for designing the cover. Finally, a special word of appreciation to the contributors to this book, which I hope will prove a fruitful source of ideas for all those who have to grapple with the conflict of interest problems that have become an inevitable feature of modern commercial life.

R. M. Goode

Centre for Commercial Law Studies,
Queen Mary College,
10th September 1986.

HOW CONFLICTS OF INTEREST MAY ARISE

Robert Pennington

In recent years the subject of conflicts of interest has attracted considerable attention in connection with the activities of persons engaged in financial and investment transactions in which others have interests which they are under a legal or moral duty to protect. This increased attention has been stimulated partly by the revelations of the activities of certain managing agents of underwriting syndicates at Lloyds, who have creamed off a large part of the premium income of their principals, the names, by placing reinsurance contracts with overseas companies which are controlled by the agent, and partly by the discoveries made by liquidators and receivers of certain insolvent companies when they investigated the applications the companies' directors have made of their assets. However, the main stimulant to awakening interest has been the prospect of the radical changes which will take place in the organisation of the institutions of the City of London in 1986, when single capacity functioning disappears from the Stock Exchange and at the same time legislation is brought into force to regulate City activities generally. The subject of conflicts of interest is therefore topical and material in connection with developments which are near at hand, and it is made of even greater practical import by the courts defining more precisely in recent cases the obligations of agents and others who act as representatives. The law is not the only regulator in this context, however. The professional bodies for the various sectors of the City have imposed increasingly stricter professional obligations on their members by internal rule-making, and with the establishment next year of almost universal self-regulation in the City subject to oversight by a Government appointed agency, the rules of the self-regulatory organisations (which the professional bodies will become) will become even more significant.

Degree of conflict of interest

It is fairly easy to define a conflict of interest, but much more difficult to draw a dividing line between situations where a person who acts in a representative capacity has such a substantial interest in conflict with the interests of those he represents that, under the law or the professional rules to which he is subject, he is required either to abstain from acting, or to account for any gain he has obtained if he has acted, and situations where his interest is not sufficient for such restrictions to be imposed on him. Some conflict of interest situations are so obvious that the representative clearly acts wrongfully if he prefers his own interest to that of the person he represents, or, in some cases, if he acts at all on behalf of that person. For example, an agent who accepts a bribe or secret commission from the other party with whom he negotiates a contract on his principal's behalf clearly breaches his fiduciary duties to his principal, and an agent employed to sell property or investments clearly puts himself in a conflict of interest situation if he sells the property or investments to himself or to a company which he controls. The existence of a conflict of interest is less apparent, however, when a person accepts a transfer of shares in a company from a controlling shareholder, when the transfer is intended to and does induce him to accept a directorship; the transfer can either be regarded as a secret benefit which the appointee obtains as a result of his directorship, with the result that he is accountable to the company for the value of the shares, or it can be regarded as part of the remuneration he bargains for as the price of his services. Again, directors of a company who carry on a business of their own in competition with that of the company obviously put themselves in a conflict of interest situation, but is it as certain that they do so if they use information which they obtain in the course of acting as directors to pursue a business or investment opportunity which is totally unconnected with the kind of business which the company carries on?

Interest must be substantial and relevant

In truth, the question in these marginal situations is not so much whether a conflict of interest situation exists, as whether the pursuit of the representative's private interest would or might prevent him from achieving the best results in the interest of the person he represents. If the risk is substantial, the principles of equity impose restrictions on the representative's freedom to act, and the rules of professional organisations often reinforce the equitable principles, which are necessarily general in terms, by imposing specific restrictions or requiring specific steps to be taken. The underlying principle of equity is that a person who acts as representative of another is in a conflict of interest situation if, either at the time when he accepts appointment or subsequently while he acts as a representative, there is a material interest of his own or a third person for whom he also acts, and the pursuit or protection of that interest would create a substantial risk that he might not act in the best way to pursue or protect the interest of the person he represents. The representative's interest or the third party interest must, of course, be a material one both in the sense that it must be substantial enough to be likely to influence the representative's judgment, and in the narrower sense that it must be relevant to the transaction he is to effect on behalf of the person he represents. For example, a stockbroker who is employed to buy or sell investments for a client has no conflicting interest if, as a principal, he contracts to buy a house from the client or to sell a house to him, but he may well have a conflicting interest if the market price of the investments is volatile so that it reacts sharply to individual sales or purchases and the client is either buying the investments with the proceeds of sale of his house, or is selling the investments in order to buy the house. The other feature of a conflict of interest situation, the risk that the representative may not act in the best way to promote the interests of the person he represents, to some extent overlaps the first feature, namely, the materiality of the conflicting interest, but it also has distinctive aspects of its own. Equity does not impose restrictions on a fiduciary who has an admittedly substantial interest, unless there is a real likelihood that the representative's judgment will be influenced by it. For example, the manager of a unit trust is entitled to remuneration which is proportionate to the value or income of the investments for the time being held by the trust, and so there may be some incentive for the manager to invest the fund in high yielding popular investments which carry a substantial risk as regards capital. The risk of this happening, however, is slight having regard to the limitations which unit trust deeds put on managers, and so equity does not prohibit unit trust managers taking remuneration in that form. If the manager did in fact invest the fund in risky securities which a reasonably competent manager would not have selected, and the trust fund suffers a loss in consequence, the manager will be liable for the loss either at common law for carrying out its contractual functions negligently, or in equity by way of compensation for breach of its fiduciary obligations. This liability, however, would not arise because of a conflict of interests in the manager, but because of a breach of his positive duties.

Growth of fiduciary obligations

During the last three hundred years, equity has elaborated the content of fiduciary obligations with considerable particularity, and has extended them to ever-widening categories of persons who act in a representative capacity and not exclusively on their own account. The earliest fiduciaries were trustees of express trusts, but in the course of the 18th and early 19th centuries agents, partners, company promoters and directors were brought into the net, and fiduciary duties broadly comparable to those of trustees were imposed on them. In particular they were all required positively to act in the best interests of the persons they represented (as well as in the interest of themselves if they, too, were in the position of beneficiaries), and as the corollary of this positive duty, they were required not to prefer their own personal extraneous interests or those of third parties. The sanctions which equity applies when a fiduciary puts himself in a conflict of interest situation are removal of the fiduciary from functioning (e.g. removal of a trustee, dissolution of a partnership, termination of an agency agreement), enjoining the fiduciary from carrying out a transaction which was tainted by his own conflicting interest and rescinding such a transaction if it has been carried out, requiring the fiduciary to account for any profit or gain he has made, whether as a result of preferring his own interest or not, and finally requiring the fiduciary to compensate the persons he represents for any loss they suffer as a result of the fiduciary prefering his own interest or that of a third party. These sanctions are not applied, of course, if the fiduciary makes full disclosure of the conflicting interest to the person he represents, and the latter, being of full age and capacity, consents to the fiduciary acting in the way he proposes to promote that interest. The widest category of fiduciaries to whom the equity rules apply are agents. This is because an agency relationship arises whenever one person agrees to act on behalf of another in connection with a legal transaction; no vesting of assets in the agent for the purpose of his mandate is required, as in the case of a trust, and the agency need not relate to particular functions, like those of a company promoter or director. Most commercial and financial activities in the City of London involve the employment of agents for negotiating, effecting and carrying out the whole or substantial parts of the relevant transactions, and the persons and institutions involved in such transactions are therefore subject extensively to fiduciary duties in performing their functions.

Many new cases after Big Bang!

The changes which are currently taking place in the organisation and functioning of the City of London will give rise to conflict of interest in many situations where it has not previously existed. The abolition of single capacity on the Stock Exchange will result in its members being able to act concurrently on their own behalf as well as on behalf of clients. The freedom for financial institutions to acquire up to 100 per cent holdings in Stock Exchange member firms mean that they may have as their subsidiaries firms of stockbrokers, firms of broker/dealers and firms which combine broking with market making. At the same time such institutions or financial conglomerates, as it is now becoming usual to call them, will have other subsidiaries which carry on business as merchant banks in marketing companies' securities and providing corporate financing facilities, and also subsidiaries which carry on insurance business and the management of pension funds, unit trusts and investment trust companies. Where a financial conglomerate carries on several of these different activities through departments of itself, the possibilities of conflict of interest are obvious. For example, the broking and dealing department of a conglomerate could well act for private clients in buying or selling securities of a company at the same time as the corporate finance department of the same conglomerate is arranging for the raising of capital by the company or advising it on a takeover bid, and the fund's management department is seeking to buy or sell a large block of the company's shares. The segregation of the conglomerate's multiple activities between several wholly-owned subsidiaries would not necessarily make any material difference. The risks of attending conflicts of interest would still be as great if the staff of the various subsidiaries exchanged information about transactions in which they were respectively engaged, and decisions were taken on the basis of what is of the greatest benefit to the conglomerate as a whole (including preferring the interests of its most valued clients) rather than what is the best course to take in each individual transaction for the benefit of the client to which it relates. There can be no doubt whatsoever that the courts will not regard the separate corporate personality of the subsidiaries of financial conglomerates as an obstacle to applying the equitable principles to transactions entered into by the various subsidiaries when the conglomerate as a whole is affected by a conflict of interests. This will be so particularly in situations where there is evidence of collaboration or the mutual supply of information about current transactions between different departments or subsidiaries of a conglomerate, but it is also likely that the courts will be strict in dealing with conflict of interest situations where there is evidence that there has not been a complete operational segregation of the functions of the different departments or subsidiaries and an effective embargo on communications about current transactions between them.

New rules will be necessary

Because of the unavoidable generality of the equitable principle governing the acts of representatives who have a conflict of interests, it will be necessary for the professional bodies which are to become the self-regulatory organisations under the Financial Services Bill to work out in detail the specific restrictions which need to be imposed on their members so that clients, companies whom they advise on corporate finance matters and pension and other managed funds are fairly treated and properly protected. Many of these rules already exist, such as the Stock Exchange rule requiring a broker who matches instructions to buy and sell the same security to put the matched deal through the market to ensure that the price is a fair one. Other rules will be made imperative by the changed organisation of the City, such as the proposed Stock Exchange rule that broker/dealers must give priority to unexecuted orders from clients over their own dealings and must not defer booking purchases of securities for discretionary funds they manage so as to be able to prefer one fund to another when an allocation is later made. The difficulty in settling such rules lies in the fact that the new dispensation for the City will seek to reconcile two objectives, namely, open competition between the City institutions in giving service and engaging in trans-actions for themselves, and the proper protection of clients, private investors and the beneficiaries of managed funds. The two objectives are not irreconcilable, but they will often produce conflicts, and the segregation and insulation of different parts of financial con-glomerates will not provide a universal protection for the interests of clients etc. Moreover, the imposition of rules designed to prevent conflicts of interest can result in clients etc. losing benefits which might otherwise accrue to them. However, it is probably more important that the City should be seen to be acting in accordance with proper principles than that clients etc. should get the best available bargain in every case.

CONFLICTS OF INTEREST AND THE CITY REVOLUTION

Jim Gower

Conflicts of interest have always been with us and are inevitable in what it is now fashionable to call the financial services industry. All that is remarkable is the complacency with which the City of London has formerly viewed them. Recent events, however, have exposed, and thereby jolted, that complacency. The most conspicuous and disturbing of these events occurred in relation to one of the City's most famous institutions – Lloyd's of London – and revealed that some of its members had engaged in practices which enabled them to make secret profits at the expense of the members of their syndicates and that at the time hardly any of their colleagues would have realised that such behaviour was in any way improper.

These and other revelations coincided with what is popularly called 'the City Revolution' – a not inaccurate description because the UK is now in the process of transforming inside three years its financial services and their regulation so as to catch up with, and, in some respects, to go further than, developments which have taken place gradually over three or more decades in the world's other major financial centres. The catalyst that brought about this rapid transformation was the out-of-court settlement in 1983 of the reference by the Director-General of Fair Trading of the rules of the Stock Exchange to the Restrictive Trade Practices Court. These rules were, clearly, restrictive of competition – as the rules of any exchange inevitably are to some extent. Whether those of the Stock Exchange were *unreasonably* restrictive was arguable – though it was difficult to argue that the best way of resolving the argument was to subject a 500 page rule-book to the scrutiny of a court of law operating under our traditional adversarial system. Belatedly, after the preliminaries had dragged on for four years (during which the Exchange was understandably reluctant to make any rule-changes lest that should weaken its case), the Government and the Exchange sensibly agreed that the reference should be stayed on the basis that the Exchange would amend its rules to the satisfaction of the Secretary of State for Trade and the Governor of the Bank of England.

It is an undoubted fact that no one at the time foresaw how far-reaching the results would be. Nevertheless, it was recognised that the Stock Exchange's rules, on membership and ownership of member firms, on 'single capacity' (the enforced separation of 'job-

7

bers' making markets as principals and of 'brokers' acting as agents for investors) and on fixed minimum commissions, inhibited the City from playing a full role in the world-wide movement from small specialised partnerships to large limited liability and well-capitalised incorporated conglomerates offering a full range of financial services. Because of the near-monopoly of the Stock Exchange of the primary and secondary market in securities and the relative unimportance of the over-the-counter market, member firms – both brokers and jobbers – were essential parts of fully effective UK financial conglomerates and it was foreseen that the agreed rule-changes would facilitate their growth. But what was not foreseen was that within a few months nearly all the major member-firms would become, in effect, wholly-owned subsidiaries of other financial institutions – British, foreign or multinational – and that by the Big Bang in the autumn of 1986 single capacity, as well as minimum commissions, would also be things of the past. Indeed, the full extent of what has happened even before the Big Bang is still not fully realised. *Legally* member-firms are not yet wholly-owned subsidiaries – since the Stock Exchange's rules have not yet been changed to permit the holding by outside institutions of more than 29.9% of their capital. In most cases, however, the 'parent' financial institution has acquired that proportion and obtained an option to acquire the remaining 70.1% when the rules are amended to permit that. For all practical purposes control has been obtained, in most cases some two years before the impending Big Bang.

The proliferating financial conglomerates in many cases include a full range of financial services – stockbroking and market-making, dealings in futures and options, insurance and insurance broking, banking, investment management and advice, the operation of unit trusts and mutual funds and corporate finance – as well as allied services such as estate agency and executor and trusteeship. This undoubtedly increases the risk of conflicts of interest and of their abuse. One of the many papers on such conflicts, which have been published by the CSI (now defunct), the Stock Exchange, the Bank of England, the DTI, and the embryo Securities and Investments Board, identified no less than 14 situations of conflicts which might arise in relation to a single transaction undertaken by such a conglomerate.

Of the two remaining main changes of the Stock Exchange's rules – abolition of single capacity and of minimum commissions – the latter is neutral as regards conflicts of interests but the former will add a further dimension. The abolition was not required by the Government or the Bank of England; on the contrary, they encouraged the Stock Exchange to retain it for as long as possible, recognising that it was a valuable protection against self-dealing to the detriment of investors. But the Stock Exchange has always argued that single capacity could not survive the abolition of fixed commissions and the Exchange accordingly decided to abolish it too. Even if fixed commissions were not abolished, the continued viability of single capacity would be very dubious. The contraction in the number of jobbing firms, the growing internationalisation of investments and American competition were ringing its death knell and already the Stock Exchange has had to recognise exceptions when it need not apply, notably in connection with international dealings. Nor must it be forgotten that single capacity is unique to the Stock Exchange and a few overseas stock exchanges located in countries to which we exported it when they were parts of our colonial empire. Furthermore, it has no application to any of London's futures and options exchanges. Nor is single capacity on the Stock Exchange, as some of the discussion has tended to suggest, a long-standing institution introduced with a view to investor protection; in fact it was a 20th century introduction designed to protect the market makers. Its abolition will not add a new type of conflict; it will merely widen the scope of a familiar conflict situation.

The City Revolution is often described as "de-regulation". This is somewhat misleading. What in fact is occurring is the enforced removal of anti-competitive restrictions and barriers (mostly self-imposed), but coupled with the introduction of increased and more comprehensive statutory regulation and surveillance of self-regulation to protect the public against the increased risk of abuse of the resulting conflicts of interest.

This new regulation will, under the Financial Services Bill, now before Parliament, be a system best described as self-regulation within a statutory framework and subject to surveillance by an independent practitioner-based body, performing much the same functions as the Securities and Exchange Commission (and the Commodity Futures Trading Commission) of the USA but dressed up in such a way as to persuade the City that it will not resemble the SEC too closely.

The practitioner-based body will be formed by a merger of the two embryo bodies (the Securities and Investments Board and the Marketing of Investments Board) and among its tasks will be that of finishing the work that these two bodies have already been engaged on for many months – that of producing rules and regulations to prevent the abuse of conflicts of interest and other misbehaviour and to monitor and enforce the observance of these rules (which those of its self-regulatory organisations will have to mirror if these SROs

9

are to be 'recognised'). In contrast with the present horse-and-buggy system (or lack of system) under the Prevention of Fraud (Investments) Act, virtually all those carrying an investment business (widely defined) will have to satisfy the body or one of its SROs that they are 'fit and proper' to undertake that business and will be subject to stringent rules in their conduct of it. The City Revolution consists not only of de-regulation but also of effective and comprehensive regulation which, it is hoped, will protect investors against both the fraudulent and the incompetent.

Some of the recent media coverage has given the impression that prevention of fraud is the primary aim of the proposed legislation. That is not so. Nor is it true that the City of London was formerly as pure as driven snow but has now become a den of thieves. More effective prosecution of fraudsters is undoubtedly needed and it is greatly to be hoped that the recommendations of the Roskill Committee will be speedily implemented. The Financial Services Bill has a different aim – the protection of investors by preventing incompetence and misconduct, as well as fraud which generally (not always) results from initial incompetence rather than from long-term planning.

Regulation of behaviour in situations of conflicts of interest is one of the major problems that will have to be solved. This conference, therefore, was timely; banks in particular will be up to their necks in such situations.

CONFLICTS OF INTEREST: LEGAL RULES AND EQUITABLE PRINCIPLES

Terence Prime

1 INTRODUCTION

From a lawyer's point of view it is perhaps easiest to begin an analysis of the legal rules affecting conflicts of interest in banking from the basis of the three underlying legal situations which may underpin any conflict of interest situation, for from that variety flow the different legal consequences which may obtain. The three situations are as follows:

(1) No legal connection

Here there is no pre-existing legal connection between the banker and the person with whom his interests conflict. That person is not the customer of his bank. The bank's activities are undertaken purely for the purposes of the bank and not for those of the other person. An example would be the taking of a guarantee from a non-customer to secure the overdraft of a customer. Here there is no legal connection between banker and guarantor prior to the signing of the guarantee and therefore no contract to define the bank's duties to the guarantor prior to the signing of the guarantee. In these circumstances any duties which do arise can only do so because the law imposes them by implying a fiduciary relationship between the bank and its prospective guarantor. The extent to which the law will impose such fiduciary responsibilities (if at all) is considered later in this paper.

(2) A purely contractual relationship where the bank is not the agent of its customer

The second situation which can arise is where there is a legal relationship between the bank and the person with whom its interests conflict because that person is the customer of the bank, but the relationship is one of simple contract and the bank is not the agent of the customer. Examples would be where the banker takes a guarantee from a customer to secure the overdraft of another customer or where, having held itself out as competent to give proper professional investment advice, it gives such advice to a customer. Here there is

11

no agency as the bank is not mandated to take any action on behalf of the customer, but the bank is in a contractual relationship with the customer. In part that relationship will be defined by the terms of the contract, which may be express or implied (e.g. into the contract between the bank and its customer to whom advice is given with regard to investment, there will be implied a term that reasonable skill and diligence will be exercised by the bank in preparing the advice which it gives). Thus the responsibilities of the bank in its dealings with its customer where there is a conflict of interest will be largely defined by the terms of the contract between them, although the law may impose fiduciary responsibilities over and above the contract, as in the first situation considered.

(3) The bank the agent of its customer

Finally the bank may be mandated to take action on behalf of its customer with whom its interests conflict, when the full status of agency is created, with the bank the agent of the customer. Examples would include where the banker is mandated to make investments on behalf of the customer (perhaps pursuant to a discretion conferred upon the bank e.g. as to the prices between which particular shares may be purchased), or where a bank is appointed fiscal agent on a Eurobond issue with defined duties to be carried out on behalf of the issuer. Here again much of the responsibility imposed upon the bank in the event of a conflict of interest will arise from the contract itself, as in the case of situation (2) above, but since the contract of agency is a long-established legal category of contract, definite terms of a fiduciary nature have come to be implied into the contract over many years, with the result that the fiduciary responsibilities of the bank where its own interests conflict with those of its customer are more clearly defined than in the first two situations considered. For this reason it is worth distinguishing category (3) as a separate category from category (2).

There is another reason why it is worthwhile doing this. Conflicts of interest may arise in two distinct ways:
(a) the bank's interest may be in conflict with the person with whom it is dealing, whether that person is a customer or not;
(b) the bank has two customers for whom it is responsible whose interests are in conflict. In this situation the bank itself has no axe to grind but must discharge its conflicting duties to its two customers. Conflicts of interest of type (b) usually arise in the third situation where the bank has a discretion and mandate to operate on behalf of its two customers in relation to each of

which it stands as agent. By contrast conflicts of interest of type (a) can arise in all three situations, but are currently giving rise to the greatest difficulty in the first two, particularly with regard to the taking of guarantees and securities from third parties to secure the indebtedness of a customer.

In considering these three situations, (2) will be taken first, as the law applicable to situation (1) is best understood in the light of that applicable to (2).

2 CONTRACTUAL RELATIONSHIP BUT NO AGENCY

Nature of the contract

In this situation a contract exists between the banker and its customer under which the banker provides banking services to its customer. The terms of the contract may be express; more often its terms will arise from implication. The position of the bank is simply governed by strict common law contractual rules. Therefore if the interests of the bank conflict with those of the customer the bank is not released from its contract with its customer. It must still fulfil its contractual obligations under general contractual principles. Thus if the bank having advertised its competence to give investment advice accepts a commission from a customer to advise the customer on the customer's investment, it is not absolved from its responsibility to give honest and competent investment advice merely because the bank feels the need to diversify the holding of its share capital. If it feels that its own share price is standing at too high a level, or in some other respect the shares do not meet the particular needs of this individual customer, it necessarily follows that the bank cannot serve its own interests by recommending investment in its shares, and if it proceeds to do so it stands in breach of its contract and at risk in an action by its customer.

Over and above the common law rules, equity grants a remedy in addition to the contractual obligations, which offers some protection to the customer where a conflict of interests arises between banker and customer. This is necessary because the contract between banker and customer may be drawn up by the bank, in express terms, in such a way as to confer no rights upon the customer at all and merely place obligations upon him in favour of the bank. The most obvious case of this is where the bank takes a guarantee or security from one customer to secure its lending to another. Here the customer giving the guarantee or security is not directly benefiting from the legal transaction being undertaken. The means utilised by the courts to give some protection is the equitable doctrine of undue influence.

The principles of undue influence

The principles under which equity will intervene were set out in the case of *Lloyds Bank Ltd* v. *Bundy*[1], which has recently been considered by the House of Lords in *National Westminster Bank plc* v. *Morgan*[2]. In Bundy's case the majority[3] of the court held that the relationship between bank and customer had developed to such an extent that what it termed 'a relationship of confidence' had arisen. Emphasising that normally the relationship of banker and customer is simply a commercial relationship, the court held that nevertheless this could develop to the extent that if a conflict of interest arose, undue influence might be inferred in the absence of evidence to show that the customer had been able to form an independent and informed judgment, which would normally require independent advice from a man of affairs.

In Bundy's case the protection given to the customer was said to be a matter of public policy so that if the confidential relationship arose the duty of the bank was to ensure that the decision of its customer was an informed and free one. In *Morgan's Case* the House of Lords held that the Court of Appeal had been wrong on this point in *Bundy* and that the true basis of the court's approach should be to prevent the victimisation of one party by another. Consequently the court would only intervene to set aside a transaction which was manifestly to the disadvantage of the customer. For this reason the customer in *Morgan's Case* failed, as she had received a substantial advantage in that the charge she and her husband had given was in the nature of a rescue operation in respect of their home which was threatened with repossession from their existing mortgagees. The wife had obtained time and the opportunity for the husband to make a success of his financial affairs, which would have resolved their problem. On this basis the case was distinguished from *Bundy's Case* where the customer received no obvious advantage, since the transaction was designed to secure an overdraft which had already been allowed to rise to an unsatisfactory level.

---

1. [1974] 3 All ER 757; [1975] 1 QB 327, discussed by C Carr (1975) 38 MLR 463.
2. [1985] 1 All ER 821. See the case note by D. Tiplady (1985) 48 MLR 579.
3. Sachs and Cairns LJJ.

Perhaps the most important question arising from these two cases is the degree of closeness of relationship between banker and customer necessary to give rise to the operation of equitable intervention. The court in *Bundy's Case* was very careful to place the equitable principle in a distinctly practical background and it is perhaps this above all which is necessary to an understanding of the case.

'What happened on December 17 1969, has to be assessed in the light of the general background of the existence of the long-standing relations between the Bundy family and the bank. It not infrequently occurs in provincial and country branches of great banks that a relationship is built up over the years, and in due course the senior officials may become trusted counsellors of customers of whose affairs they have an intimate knowledge. Confidential trust is placed in them because of a combination of status, goodwill and knowledge. [The assistant manager] was the last of a relevant chain of those who over the years had earned or inherited such trust whilst becoming familiar with the finance and business of the Bundys and the relevant company.'[4]

3 NO CONTRACTUAL RELATIONSHIP

In this situation there is no pre-existing customer relationship and therefore no contractual duty for the bank to discharge, unless duties are imposed by the bank under the terms of the transaction itself. As the most likely situation where this relationship will arise is the giving of a charge or guarantee by a non-customer to secure the borrowing of a customer, it is unlikely that under the terms of the charge or guarantee any significant contractual rights will be conferred on the non-customer. Any rights must therefore arise from the intervention of equity.

In considering equity's position a fundamental issue arises. For equity to intervene is it necessary that there should be a bank-customer relationship? Is it necessary for a confidential relationship to arise that such a contractual relationship should already exist? In *O'Hara* v. *Allied Irish Bank*[5] Harman J took the view that it was. Further one has to accept that the long-established relationship between bank and customer on which old Mr Bundy relied was a

4. [1974] 3 All ER at p.769 [1975] 1 QB at p.345.
5. [1985] B.C.L.C. 52.

vital factor in the decision of that case. Since *Morgan's Case* indicates a more restrictive approach than that of *Bundy*, it does now seem clear that the pre-existing relationship is necessary and influence will not be assumed because of the professional status of the bank-manager and the apparent dependence of a signatory such as old Mr Bundy.[6]

4 BANK THE AGENT OF THE CUSTOMER[7]: CONFLICTING INTERESTS OF AGENT AND PRINCIPAL

The bank's contractual duty

The underlying basis of the agency relationship is contractual and in general its terms will be dictated by the contents of the contract, set against strict common law contractual rules. It follows that, as in the general bank-customer relationship, the bank is required to perform the obligations it contracted to discharge as agent, even though its own interests may conflict. If it contracts to produce a result it must produce that result. More usually the implication will be simply that in carrying out its mandate on behalf of the customer the bank contracts that it will do so with reasonable skill and care.

The fiduciary aspect of agency: a general consideration

However the relationship is not entirely circumscribed by its origins in contract with its strong common law basis. As has been well-stressed 'agency is both a general principle of the law of contract and at the same time a special contract'.[8] It is a contract to which, as in other specialist fields, the law has attached certain defined responsibilities and rights. In particular the relationship between agent and principal like that of trustee and beneficiary, is fiduciary but with the 'crucial distinction ... that the agency relationship is personal; the trust relationship proprietary'.[9] The consequence of the

6. Any responsibility of the bank thus arises independently of the conflict of interest, such as where it uses an intermediary who exercises influence as in *Avon Finance Co.* v. *Bridger* [1985] 2 All ER 281, or influence is used independently by some other person to the knowledge of the bank *Bainbrigge* v. *Brown* (1881) 18 ChD 188 at p.197.
7. As by carrying out some mandate e.g. the management and investment of funds.
8. G.H. Treitel *An Outline of the Law of Contract* (3rd ed.) p.239.
9. R.H. Maudsley and E.H. Burn *Trusts and Trustees: Cases and Materials* (3rd edn.) pp.7–8.

fiduciary nature of the relationship of trustee and agent is that considerable responsibilities are placed upon the agent. It has been written with regard to these duties that 'they are equitable in character and may be lumped together under one general principle, namely that the agent must not let his own personal interest conflict with the obligations he owes to his principal'.[10] Such a general idea is, of necessity, manifested in a number of ways. The agent may not purchase his principal's property for his own purpose, or sell to the principal his own property. If the agent breaches this obligation, the principal may either repudiate the transaction altogether, or adopt it and claim for himself the benefit made by his agent.[11] These consequences could only be avoided by a full disclosure of the transaction and its circumstances, including details of the real value of the property concerned, so that it is demonstrated that it was entered into with the full and informed consent of the principal.[12] Similarly an agent must not make a secret commission. Nor may he make a secret profit out of any property of his principal, which has been entrusted to him, or from opportunities arising from their fiduciary position.[13] If however the taking of commission is normal and notorious in a particular set of circumstances (e.g. the sharing of commission by a bank with stockbrokers on making an investment for a customer) it may be that either the fiduciary duty is waived in respect of the particular commission, or the duty exists but is not breached because the commission payment, being notorious, is not secret.[14]

10. G.H. Fridman *The Law of Agency* (5th ed.) pp.152–3.
11. See the remarks of Romilly M.R. in *Bentley* v. *Craven* (1853) 18 Beav. 74 at p.76.
12. See the remarks of Lord Hodson in *Boardman* v. *Phipps* [1967] 2 AC 46.
13. *Boardman* v. *Phipps* supra; *Shallcross* v. *Oldham* (1862) 2 J and H 609. A secret profit is one made where disclosure by the agent to his principal is inadequate and therefore does not necessarily connote moral turpitude. In *Boardman* v. *Phipps* it was recognised that the solicitor agent had exercised a degree of diligence far in excess of that required of an agent and no attempt to conceal the agent's activities from the principal had been made. Indeed the solicitor agent was awarded remuneration for his services on a generous basis.
14. *Hippisley* v. *Knee* [1905] 1 KB 1 at p.9; cf. *Brown* v. *I.R.C.* [1964] 3 All ER 119.

The flexibility of equity

It would, however, be dangerous to regard fiduciary obligations in narrow defined terms; there is no reason why, if faced with a breach of the confidence of the relationship, equity should not fall back on the general idea to give a remedy. Indeed such is the flexibility of the equitable approach, that it is by no means certain that the full panoply of fiduciary obligations and remedies will be automatically implied into every agency relationship. Thus, in the US, Frankfurter J. has cryptically summarised the position as follows:

'To say that a man is a fiduciary only begins analysis; it gives direction to further inquiry. To whom is he a fiduciary? What obligations does he owe as a fiduciary? In what respect has he failed to discharge these obligations? And what are the consequences of his deviation from duty.'[15]

A similar point has been made in the English courts.

'It is said that the son ... was in fiduciary relationship to his mother. This illustrates in a most striking form the danger of trusting to verbal formulae. Fiduciary relations are of many different types; they extend from the relation of myself to an errand boy who is bound to bring me back my change up to the most intimate and confidential relations which can possibly exist between one party and another where the one is wholly in the hands of the other because of his infinite trust in him. All these are cases of fiduciary relations, and the Courts have again and again, in cases where there has been a fiduciary relation, interfered and set aside acts which, between persons in a wholly independent position would have been perfectly valid. Thereupon in some minds there arises the idea that if there is any fiduciary relation whatever any of these types of interference is warranted by it. They conclude that every kind of fiduciary relation justifies every kind of interference. Of course that is absurd. The nature of the fiduciary relation must be such that it justifies the interference. There is no class of case in which one ought more carefully to bear in mind the facts of the case, when one reads the judgment of the Court on those facts, than cases which relate to fiduciary and confidential relations and the action of the Court with regard to them.'[16]

15. *S.E.C.* v. *Chenery Corporation* 318 US 80, 85-86 (1943).
16. *Re Coomber, Coomber* v. *Coomber* [1911] 1 Ch. 723 at 728–9.

This, of course, does little to analyse the precise situations in which the fiduciary obligations arise and their extent where applicable. The courts have been less than precisely analytical in their dealings with this problem. One of the most exhaustive academic surveys suggests a general theory of fiduciary obligation in terms of the transfer of the encumbered power, namely that 'a fiduciary relationship exists whenever any person acquires a power of any type on condition that he also receives with it a duty to utilise that power in the best interests of another and the recipient of the power uses that power.[17] Essentially such a power is discretionary in nature and as a result necessitates the reliance of the donor upon the skill and integrity of the donee. In general the incidence and extent of the fiduciary obligation will be related to these factors.

The historical development of the fiduciary obligations into the agency relationship undoubtedly was by way of implication into those particular relationships where the discretion was particularly intense and the need for the obligations most extreme. However the situation of the modern law seems to be that fiduciary obligations arise as a general rule in all agency relationships although their incidence and extent vary with the nature of the specific agency concerned[18] and lead to the difficulty that cases ultimately often depend on their particular facts and that judges find it very easy to disagree on the fiduciary implications of the same facts.[19]

The consequences of breach of fiduciary duty

In general, where the fiduciary obligations of an agent are breached by his allowing his own interests to conflict with those of his principal, various consequences follow. Any secret profit or commission can be recovered from the agent, the contract of agency can be determined forthwith, the agent is no longer entitled to his *agreed* commission and any transaction entered into with a third party who knew of the irregularity can be set aside.[20] The agent is required to keep his own property separate from that of his principal[21], and may be called on

---

17. J.C. Shepherd *The Law of Fiduciaries* at p.96.
18. *Boardman* v. *Phipps* supra.
19. As in *Boardman* v. *Phipps* supra. What did *Boardman* v. *Phipps* really decide apart from determining that the appeal failed?
20. *Boston Deep Sea Fishing and Ice Co.* v. *Ansell* (1888) 39 Ch. D.339; *Industries and General Mortgage Co. Ltd.* v. *Lewis* [1949] 2 All ER 573 at 575.
21. *Gray* v. *Haig* (1855) 29 Beav 219; *Clarke* v. *Tipping* (1846) 9 Beav 284.

to account to his principal in respect of all property received of his principal.[22]

Nor do his potential duties end there. Property held by an agent for his principal may be held simply as agent or as trustee. If it is held simply as agent, his responsibility is to account, but the principal lacks a proprietary interest in the property. If the agent holds as trustee he holds the principal's property or money. Thus all interest earned belongs not to the agent but to the principal[23], as will any other profits generated from its use. If the agent becomes insolvent the property remains that of the principal and is not available to the agent's creditors, and because he is beneficially entitled the principal will retain his right to trace. Finally, if the agent mixes the property with his own, the agent will be forced to surrender all within the mixed fund except that which he can prove is his own property – a draconian threat indeed.[24] Unfortunately however it is by no means easy to determine whether property is held by an agent as trustee or agent, although it has been suggested[25] that a trust may be inferred '(a) where the money or property has been specifically entrusted to the agent by the principal to hold for his benefit or to use for a specific purpose[26] and (b) where money or property has been handed to the agent by a third party to hold or convert into specific property for the benefit of his principal'.[27]

22. *Bowstead on Agency* (15th ed.), p.191 et seq.
23. *Brown* v. *IRC* [1965] AC 244.
24. *Lupton* v. *White* (1808) 14 Ves 432; *Cook* v. *Addison* (1869) LR 7 Eq 466.
25. *Bowstead on Agency* (15th ed.), p.162 but see note 27 infra.
26. *Brown* v. *IRC* supra; *Burdick* v. *Garrick* (1870) LR 5 Ch App 233; *Royal Norwegian Government* v. *Calcutta Marine Engineering Co.* [1960] 2 Lloyd's Rep. 431.
27. *Littlewood* v. *Williams* (1813) 6 Taunt 277; *Seagram* v. *Tuck* (1881) 18 ChD 296. *Reid* v. *Rigley* (1894) 2 QB 40. In fact the most recent (15th) edition of Bowstead recognises that this categorisation is no better than a useful indication. As it recognises, 'it is probably better to approach the matter more functionally and ask whether the trust relationship is appropriate to the commercial relationship in which the parties find themselves; whether it was appropriate that money or property should be, and whether it was, held separately, or whether it was contemplated that the agent should use the money, property or proceeds of the property as part of his normal cash flow in such a way that the relationship of debtor and creditor is more appropriate. A relevant question is whether money or property was received in pursuance of a single transaction for which the agent was appointed, or as part of a group of transactions in respect of which a general account was to be rendered later or periodically.' (p.162).

5 THE AGENT'S CONFLICTING DUTIES TO TWO PRINCIPALS

(i) In general

The agent's duty to avoid conflicts

The fiduciary obligations of an agent are not, however, limited to avoiding conflicts between his own interests and those of his principal. He must also avoid putting himself in a position where his fiduciary responsibilities to one client conflict with those owed to another. This is the principle behind the rule that an agent cannot take a commission from both vendor and purchaser when he arranges a sale, unless *both* vendor and purchaser know of both commissions and agree that both can be earned.[28] However the fullest discussion of the difficulties that can arise and the attitude of English law to those difficulties can be found in the judgment of Donaldson J. in *North and South Trust Co. v Berkeley*.[29] This case illustrates the problems that arise for commercial concerns that seek to represent potentially conflicting interests, without considering carefully whose agent they are, and consequently without realising that a conflict of interest has arisen, before it assumes insoluble proportions.

The facts arose from the previously common practice of insurance brokers, who had arranged insurance with a Lloyds syndicate for an insured, representing the interests of the insured if a claim arose, whilst also gathering information for the syndicate on which, at least in part, its decision whether to resist the claim, or settle would be made, and which might become part of the syndicate's evidence if the claim were contested. In effect the broker is acting as agent for two sets of interests which are opposed. In the particular case, the insured demanded delivery of copies of various documents, including an assessors' report, which were in the possession of the brokers who had obtained them for the syndicate. The syndicate claimed an injunction restraining delivery. Both syndicate and insured were therefore claiming that the broker had a duty to them.

Modification of the duty by usage

It was contended that there would be no breach of the brokers' obligations to the insured if no order for delivery was made. It was contended that the practice of Lloyds and the insurance brokers

28. *Fullwood v. Hurley* [1928] 1 KB 498.
29. [1971] 1 All ER 980.

which dealt with it amounted to a mercantile usage of the trade, against which background the business of the market was done and which, accordingly, had the effect of modifying the usual obligations of the agent to his principal. However, for such a market usage to have the effect of modifying the obligations of the parties, it must be shown to be notorious, certain, and reasonable. Donaldson J. was doubtful whether the practice, though general within the market, was sufficiently well-known to be notorious. He said that there was 'no evidence that any assureds who form the class of persons who enter into the contracts affected by it have ever heard of it'.[30] In any event he found the whole practice unreasonable and consequently incapable of amounting to a legal usage.

In deciding on its reasonableness Donaldson J. weighed the practical advantages in favour of it against the difficulties – in his view insuperable – preventing the potential conflicts of interest from being properly resolved. The practical problems, to which the practice was addressed, arose from the lack of facilities of the underwriters operating in a restricted physical area traditional to their business, which caused them to rely on the administrative facilities provided by the brokers. This, as the learned judge pointed out, could be redressed by Lloyds expending money on new technology. He went on:

'In the context of settlement negotiations, it is said to be a positive advantage to the assured that his broker shall have confidential information on the strength of underwriters' defence. But how can he use this information when advising his client? Again, underwriters may be denying liability on the basis of a wholly misconceived, but apparently correct, appraisal of the facts by the assessors. The broker must treat this appraisal as confidential, and is, therefore, unable to enquire from the assured whether there may not be a fallacy. And what happens if the assured, taking a pessimistic view of the strength of his claim, indicated to his broker that he is prepared to accept a low figure in settlement, when the broker, having seen the assessor's report in confidence, knows that underwriters must be prepared to settle for a high figure?

Mr. Boag assures me that part of the training of the broker is to act properly in the dual capacity, and that he has never known insurance brokers to use their dual position improperly. But how do you train anyone to act properly in such a situation? What

30. Ibid. p.990.

course of action can possibly be adopted which does not involve some breach of the duty to one principal or the other? I yield to no one in my admiration for the skill and honesty of the insurance brokers and other men of business of the City of London, but neither skill nor honesty can reconcile the irreconcilable. The watch words of the business of insurance are "uberrimae fidei", and it is astonishing that Lloyd's should have evolved a practice which renders the maintenance of the utmost good faith so fraught with difficulty.'[31]

The consequences of conflict of principals' interests

In consequence of the rejection of the argument of market usage the position of the agent fell to be decided according to the general principle expressed by Scrutton L.J. in *Fullwood* v. *Hurley*[32]:

'No agent who has accepted an employment from one principal can in law accept an engagement inconsistent with his duty to the first principal from a second principal, unless he makes the fullest disclosure to each principal of his interest, and obtains the consent of each principal to the double employment.' However whilst the agent cannot lawfully act in this way the dictum tells us little about the consequences to be attached if he does. Such an action may be inconsistent with the agent's duty but in the judgment of Donaldson J. it is not a nullity. The agent's unlawful act provides him with no defence to a claim by his true principal for compensation for loss resulting from the agent's inability, due to the conflict of duties, fully to discharge his duties to that principal. It may further provide the true principal with a cause of action against the agent for an account and payment over of any benefit which the agent has received in the course of the unlawful agency. If the agent had been employed to make a contract between his true principal and another for whom he is also unlawfully acting as agent, the true principal can avoid the resulting sale.[33] If that other principal knew of the agency and the transaction resulted in a sale, the court will, as between two principals, presume that the other principal would have bought at a higher price or would

31. Ibid. p.991.
32. [1928] 1 KB 498.
33. See the comments of Donaldson J. in *North and South Trust Co.* v. *Berkeley* supra at p.992.

have sold at a lower price to the extent of the payment he unlawfully made to the agent.[34]

(ii) The particular problem of information

If this defines the position between principal and agent, it does not deal with the problem of resolving the conflicting interests of principal and principal. It will be remembered that in the particular case of *North and South Trust Co.* v. *Berkeley* the conflicting claims were in respect of information. This is a particular problem in the commercial world where many potential conflicts of interest arise from the use or non-use of price-sensitive information.[35] Counsel for the plaintiffs had attempted to subsume the entitlements of the two principals under a general principle, namely 'if X, a third party, knowing that A is the agent of P, the principal, enters into an agreement with A involving duties which are inconsistent with those owed by A to P, then, in the absence of the fully informed consent of P, X acts at his own peril, and where there is any resulting conflict between X's interests and P's interests the law will prefer the interests of P.' Donaldson J. thought that this general proposition contained 'much that is sound' despite the fact that no authority in support was cited or known to the court. As he recognised, the law prefers P's interests to the extent of avoiding any contracts and calling X to account in relation to any commissions paid to A.[36]

It was the attempt by counsel for the plaintiffs to apply this broad general principle to the particular problem of the case that prompted judicial reaction. Counsel asserted that: 'If, knowing of A's agency for P, X passes information or documents to A relevant to matters which are the subject of that agency, X cannot complain if A complies with his duty to P to pass on that information or to show those documents to P, however confidential that information or those documents might otherwise be, unless X has obtained the fully informed consent of P to A receiving that information or those documents exclusively on behalf of X.'

34. *Re a Debtor (No, 228 of 1927)* [1927] 2 Ch. 367; *Taylor* v. *Walker* [1958] 1 Lloyd's Rep. 490.
35. On this whole subject see B.A.K. Rider 'The Fiduciary and the Frying Pan' (1978), 42 Conv. 114.
36. *North and South Trust Co.* v. *Berkeley* at p.993. It may be that this was the total extent to which Donaldson J. was agreeing to the plaintiff's principle; see M. Kay and D. Yates, 'An Unremedied Breach of Fiduciary Duty', (1972) 35 MLR 78 at p.80.

Pointing out that this assumes that it is the duty of the agent to pass on to his principal information which he would not have obtained save on terms that it would be confidential from his principal, Donaldson J. wondered how such a duty could arise since the information is not a benefit to the agent for which he would be accountable. This of course simply begs the issue that the information was obtained, and could only be obtained, by the agent in breach of his duty to his first principal. The submission of counsel for the plaintiffs that the information was *property* which the agent had wrongfully acquired in the service of the plaintiffs, was met by Donaldson J. with three counter-arguments. Firstly he doubted whether that information was property in this context. This would seem to be inconsistent with the majority of the House of Lords and the Court of Appeal in the leading case of *Boardman* v. *Phipps*.[37] Secondly, if the information was property, the property was never acquired by the brokers but was merely in their custody, presumably because they apparently only provided an administration for the underwriters and were not called on to assimilate the information for the purpose of carrying out any mandate of the underwriters. If so, such a distinction between custody and acquisition is entirely artificial and irrelevant to the majority of cases, where the agent will not merely have to obtain information, but will have to assimilate it and react to that information, in order to carry out the mandate of the principal.[38] Thirdly, Donaldson J. rejected the contention on the ground that the information, although wrongfully acquired, was not acquired in the service of the plaintiffs. In such circumstances 'the only way in which counsel's proposition might be made good is by treating the common knowledge of the underwriter and [the broker], that the one could not lawfully give and the other could not lawfully receive the information as constituting an implied waiver of the implied seal of confidentiality, with which the information is impressed'. He rejected the view that such a waiver had occurred because the underlying problem of the acceptance of the conflicting duties in this manner in the insurance business was not known to be improper by the brokers and syndicate concerned. However Donaldson J. recognised that his approach 'will not, of course, apply in future cases' because he had expressly held that the practice is unlawful.[39]

37. [1967] 2 AC 46. See the comments of Kay and Yates, *loc. cit..* p.81.
38. See the criticism of Kay and Yates, *loc. cit.* pp.81–2.
39. The earlier denunciation of this practice by Megaw J. in *Anglo-African Merchants Ltd.* v. *Bayley* [1969] 2 All ER 421 had been ignored by the

A comment on North and South Trust v. Berkeley

It is difficult to accept the reasoning of Donaldson J. in these particulars. The fact that the information was not acquired in the service of the plaintiffs seems irrelevant to the whole situation. It was certainly obtained in breach of the agent's duty to the plaintiff, which is surely the real substantive point. Further the knowledge or otherwise of principal and agent of the impropriety of their actions *as a matter of law* is a remarkable basis for a legal decision, where the usual requirement is merely that people should have knowledge solely of the relevant facts from which they have the responsibility of drawing the correct inferences as to the propriety or otherwise of their conduct. In *North and South Trust* v. *Berkeley* both the syndicate and the brokers knew that the brokers were acting for the insured when the syndicate gave instructions for the assessor's report to be obtained, and the brokers complied with those instructions. The approach of Donaldson J. has met with considerable criticism[40] and its reasoning is difficult to defend. There must be some question as to whether it will be followed in protecting information obtained in breach of an existing fiduciary duty in the future, although what the result of this would be in the event of an appeal to the Court of Appeal in its present composition, is a matter for even greater conjecture!

Indeed a more fundamental problem of Donaldson J's approach is its division of the two issues of the liability of the agent and the entitlement to the information. The agent may be prevented from giving, or required to give the information which is being demanded but either way is not discharged from his underlying obligation to the dissatisfied party whose interests he has failed to protect. This can

---

insurance industry on the basis that it was pronounced obiter dicta. Donaldson J. went out of his way to make it clear that his own categorisation of the conduct as improper was part of the essential reasoning of his decision so that it would not be possible to ignore it in this way in future. Future plaintiffs should be able to obtain the information 'on the basis of the agent as a constructive trustee of the information. Even if the information is not regarded as property there seems no reason to suppose that the equity which restrains the transmission of confidential information in breach of some confidential relationship will not equally *compel* disclosure where the information has been obtained in breach of the duty arising from such a relationship.' Kay and Yates at p.83 citing *Boardman* v. *Phipps* particularly Lord Upjohn at pp.127–128.

40. See both Rider and Kay and Yates, *loc. cit.*

hardly be a satisfactory position for the agent. Given the commercial reality which arises from the necessary commercial business of professional trusteeship of funds undertaken by merchant banks, this begs all the real issues. Merchant banks need funds to manage and equally funds need the professional management skills of the merchant banks. To say in effect that merchant banks must never undertake trusteeship of more than one such fund, or must face the consequences if they do, flies directly in the face of commercial reality. Indeed the minority in *Boardman* v. *Phipps* alone considered this situation and expressed the view that there was no general rule that information learnt by a professional trustee in the administration of a particular trust was the property of that trust and could not be used for his own benefit or the benefit of other funds for which the trustee was responsible.[41] In the words of Lord Upjohn;

'The real rule is ... that knowledge learnt by a trustee in the course of his duties as such is not in the least property of the trust and in general may be used by him for his own benefit or for the benefit of other trusts unless it is *confidential* information which is given to him (i) in circumstances which, regardless of his position as trustee, would make it a breach of confidence for him to communicate to anyone for it has been given to him expressly or impliedly as confidential, or (ii) in a fiduciary capacity, and its use would place him in a position where his duty and his interest might possibly conflict.'[42]

On this basis the restriction arising from the fiduciary obligation is simply that the information cannot be utilized if, and only if, the use of the information for other purposes has the potential to damage the interests of the fund for whom it was obtained. This has led to the suggestion that 'perhaps the best practical solution is that information that is acquired by a fiduciary in the exercise of one duty cannot be used in the furtherance of any other duty, unless such use would not damnify the principals and beneficiaries of the relationship in which or for which the information was acquired.'[43] This of course would relieve the trustee or agent from the obligation to use the information where injury could potentially occur and remove both the agent's liability and the right to the use of the information by the other funds at the same time. It does not deal

41. Viscount Dilhorne and Lord Upjohn.
42. At p.128.
43. Rider, *loc. cit.* p.128.

with the separate question of whether the other funds are entitled to demand the use of that information on their behalf where no such potential injury to the fund for which the information was obtained exists. Such a positive duty could either be denied[44] or be left to turn on general principles of negligence depending on just how onerous the duties placed upon professional trustees and agents are to be.

(iii) The management of conflicts of interest

The need for conflicts of interest management

Nevertheless despite the potential comfort to be obtained from the minority view in *Boardman* v. *Phipps,* in the particular area of the use of information banks may well wish to consider conflict of interest management on a general basis in relation to all areas of potential conflicts including, until the position has been further clarified, the acquisition of information on behalf of customers for whom the banks are agents. For the position of the agent is deeply unsatisfactory. Where neither 'principal' knows of the agent's obligation to the other and the conflict of interest to which this gave rise, these obligations will be owed to each[45] leaving the agent with the near certainty of facing one action and the possibility of two. The problem is compounded by the fact that the conflict of interest may arise after the contracts of agency have been entered into. Where the conflict is obvious prior to that time it may be avoided by the agent declining to take on the second principal – commercially a hard decision, but legally an impeccable option. However, if the conflict only develops after the two agencies have been accepted, the position of the agent is hard.

Reliance on trade usage

One possible approach could be based upon the trade usage urged upon Donaldson J. in *North and South Trust Co.* and rejected by him. It will be remembered that his ground of rejection in this case was that the practice was unreasonable and therefore incapable of amounting to usage, and he also doubted whether it was sufficiently

---

44. The solution favoured by Rider.
45. In *North and South Trust Co.* v. *Berkeley* the second person for whom the agent acted knew of the existing agency and the conflict of interest hence the first agency could identify a clear 'true' principal.

notorious to be known to the users of the market and therefore entitled to recognition. Nevertheless the implication of the approach must be that, if the practice had been well known and reasonable, it would have operated as a contractual modification of the underlying fiduciary responsibility. It follows logically therefore that, if the practice of acceptance of conflicting fiduciary duties is sufficiently well known to users of a particular banking service to be notorious, and pursued because there is no practical alternative (unlike the position in the *North and South Trust Case* itself) so that it can be pronounced reasonable, the opposite result might be obtained and the usual fiduciary obligations modified by implication, in both contracts of agency. In practice the necessary notoriety might well prove impossible to establish in most if not all such commercial banking situations.

However, positive planning and initiative by the bank may resolve the difficulty. The implications of the same basic point could be exploited by professional fiduciaries extracting agreements expressly modifying their fiduciary responsibilities with regard to conflicts of interest and the effect of their agency arrangements with regard to all the agency and trustee work they undertake. This could be done by making full and frank disclosure to both principals prior to the creation of the agencies of the possibility of a conflict of interest developing. Such disclosure must contain all relevant information known to the agent[46] – which will be limited enough when the conflict is only a possibility – but if full and frank will generally protect the agent if the principals nevertheless consent to his acting.[47]

The Unfair Contract Terms Act 1977

There is the possibility that such an arrangement might be attacked under the Unfair Contract Terms Act 1977.[48] However where full and frank disclosure has been made and the customer freely agreed to the bank proceeding despite the potential conflict of interest, it is submitted that if the bank has cause to refer to its full and frank

46. *Lindgren* v. *L and P Estates Ltd* [1968] Ch 572 *Phipps* v. *Boardman* [1965] Ch 922.
47. *Thornton Hall* v. *Wembley Electrical Appliances Ltd* [1947] 2 All ER 630; *Lindgren* v. *L and P Estates Ltd* supra.
48. For the Act to apply the customer must contract in writing on the bank's standard form terms. For further consideration of potential complications with regard to the applicability of the Act see the note by Professor B. Coote (1978) 41 MLR 312 and the comment by J.N. Adams (1978) 41 MLR 703.

disclosure and the resultant modification of its obligations it is not claiming to render a contractual performance substantially different from that which was reasonably expected of it within s.3. Neither is it claiming by reference to the modification of the contract to render no performance at all in respect of the whole or any part of its contractual obligation (the alternative basis for the operation of s.3), for the bulk of its contractual and fiduciary obligations will remain except to the extent of the specific modification. Even if this is not so, the modification will be effective to the extent that it is reasonable, that is, that it is a fair and reasonable one to be included having regard to the circumstances which were or ought reasonably to have been known to or in the contemplation of the parties when the contract was made.[49] However, such a frank disclosure should be brought very specifically to the attention of the customer, since one of the factors to be taken into account in assessing the reasonableness of any modification caught by s.3 is whether the customer knew or ought reasonably to have known of the existence and extent of the term (having regard, among other things, to any custom of the trade and any previous course of dealing between the parties).[50] This would also be a very particular consideration to the issue of whether the bank was claiming to render a contractual performance substantially different from that which was reasonably expected of it within s.3.

Conflicts management in an evolving situation

There remains one final area of potential difficulty. Whilst disclosure of the potential conflict of interest may allow an agent to act for a particular principal in circumstances where he would otherwise be in breach of his duty, it is by no means certain that a general initial disclosure of the potential conflict will absolve the agent from all further responsibility when the conflict actually arises. It may be that the particular conflict arises in an unexpected form, not contemplated by either principal or agent at the time when the disclosure was made and the agency created. Alternatively, whilst of a nature contemplated at that time, the conflict may be much more grave or serious in its repercussions than originally contemplated. It is by no means certain that in such a situation the courts would take the view that the agents's obligations were fulfilled simply by his initial general disclosure of the potential conflict. The safer course of action would be for the agent to disclose the nature and full severity of the actual

49. s.11.
50. Sched. 2.

conflict to the principal so that, if the principal so chooses, the agency relationship can be terminated by mutual agreement and the principal obtain independent assistance elsewhere. Of course if the nature of the conflict arises from the clash of conflicting interests of two or more principals, whilst disclosing the general nature and severity of the conflict the agent would need to refrain from disclosing any specific information entitled to be treated as confidential to a particular principal, as discussed earlier.

CONFLICTS OF INTEREST
AND THE ACCOUNTANCY PROFESSION

Michael Fowle

Bernard Shaw said that 'All professions are a conspiracy against the laity.' Perhaps today the accounting profession could be forgiven for believing that the business world, lawyers and government are together a conspiracy against auditors. But as a profession we maintain high professional standards of competence and probity both in the United Kingdom and across the rest of the world, so if there is a conspiracy against us, the fault is with us for not putting our case.

This is a time of change and challenge in the financial markets and change is bringing new conflicts – or at least a clearer perception of old ones. The accounting profession also is facing change and challenge which bring new perceptions of old conflicts. The risk is that we will not recognise these conflicts: if we do not recognise them, we will not cope with them. Accountants cannot avoid, or abolish, conflicts.

THE RULES

In 1982 the Institute of Chartered Accountants in England and Wales (in consultation with Scottish and Irish Institutes) issued a Guide to Professional Ethics which to some extent covers conflicts of interest. Relevant extracts are included in annex 1. In summary, the key points are:

– a member of a profession owes duties to the public and to clients which may conflict with his or her own self interest
– members must perform their work objectively and impartially, professional independence being a concept fundamental to the accountancy profession and the product of an attitude of mind characterised by integrity and objectivity
– in accepting an assignment, a member should have regard to any factors which might reflect adversely on his or her integrity or objectivity
– client information is confidential and must not be used for personal advantage
– a member in public practice should be, and be seen to be, free in each assignment (including non-audit work) of any interest which detracts from objectivity, for example: fees should not be on a

contingency basis; no practice should earn more than 15% of its fees from one client; personal relationships with client management must not be too cosy; auditors should not own shares in client companies; audit practices should not borrow from client companies; partners should not borrow from client companies (other than from clearing banks); auditors should not be receiver or liquidator in an insolvency of an audit client; and a firm should not provide both the receiver and the liquidator of a company.

THE FUNDAMENTAL ROLE OF THE PROFESSIONAL ACCOUNTANT

Accountancy is more than the recording of cash transactions. It is the recognition that cash laid out today can have benefits for tomorrow, that cash which will not be received until tomorrow has value today. The origins of the accountancy profession lie in the need to record, measure and report the financial results of commercial and trading enterprises; measuring and reporting financial results always involve conflict between those who hold differing opinions (often opinions influenced by different interests). Accountancy is the exercise of judgment – the valuation of advances in the accounts of a bank, the proper recording of inventory in the accounts of a trading company, the proper accrual of costs incurred but not paid for.

Coping with conflicts of interest is not new to the accountant. In engaging an independent accountant, what is bought is the expertise and integrity which enables him to make independent professional judgments; his stock in trade is independence. That is the essence of the audit or 'attest' function – the fundamental role of the professional accountant. In the markets of today the auditor and the reporting accountant are engaged as independent voices in the competitive commercial world.

Accountancy as a profession, and in particular auditing, is essentially a product of the nineteenth century City of London. Today's great accounting firms are successors to the London giants of the end of the last century: Ernest Cooper, William Peat, Edwin Waterhouse, Frederick Whinney – to choose four out of many. At the same time members of the new institutes of chartered accountants like Guthrie from Manchester, Lowes Dickinson from London and Marwick from Glasgow were exporting their professional skills and ethics to the United States and so beginning to build a truly international profession.

Apart from a brief period from 1844 to 1856, United Kingdom

company law did not require audited accounts until the City of Glasgow Bank was brought down by the appalling quality of its loan portfolio. Within a year this disaster led to the 1879 Companies Act, requiring the appointment of auditors for every United Kingdom banking company. It was not until 1900 that this requirement was extended to companies generally, but by then the accountancy profession was well organised, the Institutes were of high standing and the accounts of most major United Kingdom companies carried audit reports signed by professional accountants.

If the mandatory audit is only 85 years old, the requirement for an independent accountant's report in a prospectus is not even middle aged – appearing only in the 1948 Act. But once again practice had preceded law by many decades, accountants' reports having been a familiar constituent of prospectuses since the last century.

Preparation of accounts

But auditors, though accountants, had and still have no responsibility to prepare their client company's accounts. The directors have to prepare accounts – accounts which show a true and fair view of the results and state of affairs of their company. The auditor's job is to consider whether the directors have carried out this duty properly and to express their audit opinion.

The directors have to prepare their company's accounts with the disclosures required by law, whether required explicitly or whether required to enable the accounts to meet the broad need for a true and fair view. It is then for the auditors to report whether, in their opinion, those accounts accord with law.

Accounting disclosure and the auditor

There is no requirement that accounts should disclose all the information that any journalist or stockbroker or shareholder or potential shareholder or creditor might find interesting. Accounting disclosure is a moving target. The information which was accepted by the business world as providing a true and fair view twenty five years ago might not be thought to be enough to show a true and fair view today. Consider one example.

In 1957 the accounts of the British Oxygen Company won an award for accounts of a public company; they included five notes, occupying one and a half pages. The notes and accounting policies in BOC's 1984 accounts take twenty eight pages.

In 1986 (as in 1957) the fuller the disclosure, the happier the auditor. Auditors instinctively believe in public companies publishing accounts which give the fullest information practicable. Directors, on the other hand, have to manage a competitive business in a competitive world. Auditors spend a fair amount of their time telling their client companies' directors that best practice suggests proposed disclosures which are greater than those required by law. But if the directors do not wish to make a disclosure, however desirable the auditor considers it, the auditor cannot compel disclosure unless its absence means that the accounts do not show a true and fair view. They are the directors' accounts, not the auditor's accounts.

And 'a' fair view is not necessarily the only 'fair' view. Accountancy is not a precise science; it is an art of estimate and judgment. The 1879 Companies Act required 'a ... correct view'. But such precision is impossible. The accounts of modern businesses, especially complex multinational businesses, deal with complex issues. There is no single 'true and fair view' which is correct, all others being wrong. There are many judgment issues. Inevitably there is a range which is acceptable. Auditors may pitch their preference at one end of the range and management at the other, but it is directors not auditors who prepare the accounts.

This is nothing to be defensive about. It is reality. Anybody who does not understand or does not accept this fundamental, does not understand business and does not understand accountancy. A view which you believe is less fair than another is not necessarily unfair.

The auditor's role created by demand, not by law

One lesson of the past is that the independent audit, whether of annual financial statements or of the extended statements included in prospectuses, came into being because it was needed by the markets – not because it was required by law. The independent audit of financial statements developed naturally in the City of London because the commercial world needed independent audit.

Similarly, but more recently, although a published independent accountants' report was not required on a published profit forecast until 1968, leading firms of accountants were reviewing and reporting on forecasts in private reports many years earlier. For instance, some years ago I came across my own firm's internal instructions dating from the early 1950s on the review of forecasts included in prospectuses with which our name was associated.

The auditor's function in the securities markets

Auditors have a crucial function to fulfill in the securities markets. Users of information, especially the judgmental information of accountancy, need assurance that the information they are using is sound. Laws do not make men honest. Regulations do not create integrity. The Companies Acts, the Yellow Book and Accounting Standards prescribe the contents and presentation of the accounts but it is the function of the external auditors to confirm to the user of accounts that these precepts have been followed.

A strong and independent auditing profession is essential for an effective market in securities.

WHO IS THE CLIENT?

The examination of and reporting on financial information means making judgments amidst conflicts. In order to make his judgments the auditor must identify these conflicts and thus first he must identify his client.

The auditor is a principal, an officer of the company appointed by the shareholders in general meeting. His report is addressed to the shareholders, not to the directors. The auditor's client is the company of which he is an officer and, in effect, its shareholders.

A company's management is not the auditor's client. But if auditors are to audit, to do their duty by their clients, they have to work with management. This is a practical matter. Auditors to do their job need uninhibited, trusting communication from client management, a free flow of information. Legislators can legislate for free communication but free communication in real life is people and relationships; and free relationships mean confidence.

But let there be no mistake – confidence may mean friendship but it does not mean cosiness. The management/auditor relationship is professional and arms length; it must never become cosy. The management/auditor relationship needs to be a relationship of trust, a relationship which may well take a few years to build. Yet the auditor must be independent, knowledgeable and determined.

The auditor must also build a relationship with the board of directors who are responsible for the conduct of the company's business. The auditor must know his client's people, and the chairman and the board are a vital segment of those people.

If an auditor fails to create a working relationship with the management and directors of his client, a relationship of mutual respect,

37

he will find it virtually impossible to undertake a good audit. An adversarial audit is a useless audit. The audit process may be quasi-judicial, but it must never become quasi-litigious; if an audit becomes combative, it is unlikely to be effective and it certainly will not be efficient.

Yet in terms of ultimate responsibilities, it is the shareholder who is entitled to rely on the auditor and the auditor's opinion. Indeed, the auditor has a duty beyond his simple duty to the present shareholders. Surely he has a duty to any whom he can reasonably foresee are likely to rely on the accounts upon which he has reported – not only present shareholders but also creditors, future creditors and future shareholders?

So the auditor has many constituencies with whom he must work or to whom he is responsible: management, directors, shareholders, creditors, future creditors and future shareholders. Two of his constituencies are immediate and with him day to day – management and directors. The others are distant and intangible – but they are the most important – effectively they are the client.

While in law the auditor is appointed by shareholders, in practice his appointment is in the gift of the board and his fees are settled by the board or by management. Here again is conflict.

If the auditors' duty is not only to shareholders, but also to potential shareholders and to existing and potential creditors, far more so is the directors' duty. Indeed, it is especially the non-executive directors of a public company who have a particular responsibility to the indefinable body of outsiders who invest in or are creditors of a company. And so the non-executive directors have a vital role in reviewing and judging the auditors in their duty and in examining the relationship between auditors and management. If the non-executive directors don't know how the auditors fulfil their function, they should find out. It is essential that this responsibility is taken seriously, as a continuing concern.

Even though the auditor's appointment is annual, the safeguards provided by the Companies Acts theoretically give him considerable protection; the auditor is the servant of the shareholders and must be protected from capricious management or weak directors. Such protection must be beneficial to the service that the auditor provides to the markets. But it brings with it a detriment. It brings potential inertia in the auditor's office; in the past, inadequate auditors have sometimes been able to rely on that inertia and so retain their position.

The audit as a commodity?

In recent years things have changed, in many ways for the better. We auditors know that in order to retain our clients, we must provide value for money; excellent. On the other hand some circles characterise the audit as a commodity; pity. If the audit is a commodity and if in truth there is no discernible difference between an audit report from Alpha & Co, from Beta & Co, or from Gamma & Co, these firms can be differentiated only on price; thus directors are entitled, almost obliged, to recommend to the shareholders the auditor which claims it will cost the company the least.

But in reality there is clear differentiation between different firms of auditors. Every firm depends upon its people and its culture. One individual's perception of a particular firm must depend on whom he has met and the work he has seen them do, but overall the markets' perceptions of a firm depend on reputation accumulated over many years. In the words of P. G. Wodehouse:

'Jeeves's reputation as a counsellor has long been established among the cognoscenti, and the first move of any of my little circle on discovering themselves in any form of soup is always to roll round and put the thing up to him. And when he has got A out of a bad spot, A puts B on to him. And then, when he has fixed up B, B sends C along ... And so on, if you get my drift, and so forth.

'That's how these big consulting practices like Jeeves's grow.'

Successful practices grow from their reputation. And not only from their reputation for skilful, swift and innovative service; their reputation for independence also matters. Not so long ago the Chief Executive of the National Westminster Bank said '... One thing that a good auditor and a good banker have in common is the ability to say "no" to the client and yet keep him as a client.'

If you are to say 'no' to large clients, it helps to be large. But, much more important, it is essential to have a culture that is rooted in independence and professionalism. Successful audit firms must develop – they cannot stand still, and the foundation of their development is the creation of a culture of independence and professionalism. When they have laid that foundation they can build on it to grow to the mass that is needed to enable them to retain their independence and strength.

Incidentally, saying 'no' is not always the difficult option for an auditor. Sometimes it can be safe and easy, but wrong, to disagree with the board, to say 'no'. The most conservative judgment is not necessarily the best judgment – even though in times of great difficulty it is almost always the safest course in the auditor's own immediate interest. Sometimes you need to be strong and independent to say 'yes'. The safe judgment can also be the weak judgment and the wrong judgment.

The audit committee

Just as the external auditor has to be able to live with conflict in making professional judgments, so sometimes do the chairman and the finance director and the board when they think about their auditors. Firms of auditors are different. They can be distinguished. There are style differences, personality differences and quality differences. The audit is not a commodity. 'Never mind the quality, feel the width' is no way to choose the auditors who will serve the shareholders.

Perhaps the most effective way for directors to review and consider the audit and the auditors and their relationship with management is through a properly organised audit committee of non-executive directors. No competent auditor ever fears a competent audit committee or begrudges time to it. A good audit committee provides the auditor with a surrogate for the diffuse and uncertain body of shareholders and creditors – a surrogate which can directly review, consider and evaluate his work.

An audit committee is no excuse for or defence from an inadequate audit. It provides the auditor with a forum for discussion of issues and gives him an opportunity to air his concerns, to air any differences he may have with the client management which, though real, are not so great that they have an immediate or material impact on the accounts. The good audit committee brings strength to the non-executive directors and at the same time gives the auditor greater strength to make his judgments soundly.

FINANCIAL INTERESTS IN CLIENT COMPANIES

When auditors first were imported into legislation by the 1844 Joint Stock Companies Act they tended to be shareholders who employed accountants to help them in their work. Articles of Association often specified an auditor's qualifying shareholding. Indeed, the formal professional rules which forbid auditors to be investors in their audit clients are barely ten years old, although some firms have included such prohibitions in their house rules for longer than any one can remember.

It is easy to see the rationale for the prohibition of auditors' shareholdings. There must be no risk that auditors could be suspected of enriching themselves by turning a blind eye to fudged accounts.

And so the rules are almost draconian. For example annex 2 gives extracts from Peat Marwick's rules for partners and managers. In summary we (and our dependent children and, to the extent that they comply with our requests, our spouses) may not hold any shares or other securities in any company based anywhere in the world if Peat Marwick is auditor of any material part of it.

And if you cannot yourself invest in your audit client, you cannot advise others so to invest. Your knowledge of your audit client's affairs is privileged knowledge, confidential knowledge. You cannot risk the conflict that duty to one client, the investor, may pull you to breach the duty of confidentiality to another client, the audit client.

So years ago those of the larger accounting firms which ran investment management businesses spun them off. Apparently no Chinese walls were thought to be high enough, wide enough or impervious enough to divide the auditors from the investment managers.

The prohibition on investing in clients does not itself dispose of the auditor's interest in a client's success. A professional firm is committed to the success of its clients in a very positive way without there being a need for any direct financial interest. The success of any professional firm is influenced, often significantly, by association with the success of its clients.

Here is a conflict of interest. How can you divorce the success of an auditing firm from the success of its clients? Change auditors every year or so? or create an Audit Department as an arm of state? Surely both alternatives are absurd. Some conflicts cannot be avoided – they have to be managed.

NON-AUDIT WORK FOR AUDIT CLIENTS

The auditor is a principal, not an agent nor an adviser. Although his contractual client is the company, it is third parties (shareholders, creditors, potential shareholders, potential creditors) who may rely on the auditor's opinion, given as a principal. They are entitled, if they so wish, to distinguish between one auditor's name and another's, between one firm's reputation and another's.

But as well as their principal's role to attest the accounts, auditing firms have other roles. Management and directors need to be able to use the auditor as adviser. A major auditing firm has good people with a wide experience of a diversity of businesses. It knows its client's business. In order to build its strength and its skill as a firm of auditors it has established expertise in many matters that are relevant to the client's business.

It is therefore natural and inevitable that directors will look for advice to a firm of auditors competent in their company's industry. If your audit clients never seek your advice, the chances are you are not a very good auditor.

Strength brings independence

So what is meant by 'the independent auditor'? It means more than merely that the auditor may not be a shareholder. It does not mean that you may not give advice. When discussing this issue it is difficult to avoid seeming trite. Independence is a state of mind.

In order to be the auditor of a complex group operating in many financial businesses in many countries, the auditor also must operate in many countries and must have people with many skills and specialities. In particular, a global securities market requires a global auditing profession. A strong securities market needs a strong auditing profession – a profession that can make and be seen to make independent judgments.

The auditing profession went multi-national when its first clients went multi-national, long before the First World War, and it is no accident that the great auditing firms have in general built up substantial consultancy arms.

The prime business of an auditor is the examination of financial information and the expression of an independent opinion on that information. Similarly the prime function of a management consultant is to examine a set of facts or circumstances and express his opinion, making recommendations, based on these facts and circumstances.

Unless a firm of auditors has access within itself to a wide range of skills and specialities, it is not properly equipped to fulfill its main function. Auditors of major concerns require to be strong and independent. Their consulting activities contribute to their strength and independence – and enhance the depth and the quality of the audit service they deliver.

The conflict in consultancy

But consultancy gives rise to questions about independence – it can create a conflict of interest. Can you advise directors, can you put in an information system, can you make recommendations on board level strategy, and then purport to be independent when you audit the results of your advice?

There is no simple answer, but it is a question that every audit firm must ask itself continually when it undertakes non-audit work for an audit client. There is no logic in suggesting that an auditor should refuse on principle to do non-audit work for an audit client or that an auditor should be prevented by law from doing so. That would truly be throwing out the baby with the bath water.

There are great benefits to the markets from using auditing firms with the skills and resources that come with their taxation, consulting and insolvency practices; there is no benefit in a rule which would result in everybody taking in everybody else's washing.

The importance of the attest function

But every audit firm must remember that however pleased they may be with the growth of their non-audit work, auditing is their fundamental line of business. The most important job that we do, the function which we undertake that is vital for the business world, is the audit, the attest function. The remainder of our practice gives us strength and makes us able to be better auditors, but is incidental to our main function.

The auditor must remember that his prime function is the audit and that his prime client is the shareholder/creditor client. Any other work that he undertakes for an audit client company must never be allowed to interfere with his independence of mind.

CLIENTS IN CONFLICT

If an auditing firm has the size, the mass, that gives it the strength to be independent, its client list will mean that it will from time to time face the problem of acting for two separate companies who are themselves in conflict – bidder and target.

If a firm is auditor to both bidder and target in a bid situation, it has a distinct but real duty to act for each company, to report on forecasts and cash flows (whether publicly or privately) to check figures in documents and to advise generally. The directors and management of both companies know that the firm is acting for both parties, using separate teams within Chinese walls. If both companies are happy, it serves neither to abandon both. If one company is unhappy at the concept of the firm serving both, the unhappy company should appoint another firm to review its forecasts.

Lawyers find an insoluble conflict in advising two clients in conflict and are sometimes troubled when accountants seem to take a contrary view. But the auditor is a principal whose job is to make judgments – he is not in essence an adviser (though during a bid he may provide advice as a by-product of his main function). The continuing nature of the auditor's involvement with the client is vital background to his ability to make judgments, especially judgments on issues like forecasts. It could be damaging to a company's interests to have to employ a new accountant, not the auditor, to review forecasts in a hostile bid situation.

This is not a simple matter of the relative competence of different auditing firms – the issue is that an auditor knows and knows about his client company. To make judgments on forecasts you need a background of knowledge and experience of the company, its business and its management. To deprive your audit client of that knowledge and experience at the behest of another client would be unprofessional and unacceptable.

AUDITORS AND SUPERVISORS

What should be the relationship between an auditor and a supervisory authority? This issue created a lively controversy in the United Kingdom during 1985 and the discussion was renewed following the issue in December 1985 of the Department of Trade and Industry's Consultative Document 'The Auditor's Role in the Financial Services Sector'.

If the board of directors of a company, or even better the Audit Committee, is a surrogate for its shareholders, surely the supervisory authority can be regarded as a surrogate for its creditors and potential creditors – not only depositors but also clients and customers (who may be or become creditors)?

It is essential for there to be a relationship of understanding and co-operation between the management, supervisors and auditors of any company which is subject to prudential supervision in the financial services sector. But the roles of the auditors and the supervisors need to be clearly distinguished.

In fulfilling their responsibility to report on the accounts the auditors are concerned primarily with matters which they consider could materially affect the view presented by the accounts. The supervisors are concerned to protect the public interest by establishing prudential and other guidelines for the management of the business. To support their function, the supervisors need to have regular contact with and receive regular reports from the management.

Supervisors must be entitled to rely upon the auditor's report on the accounts. But the supervisors need to have a clear understanding of the nature and extent of the auditor's work so that they can assess how far it assists them in discharging their supervisory responsibilities. Supervisors must also be entitled to obtain specific reports from auditors on financial information supplied to them by management and on the client's compliance with specified requirements of the supervisors. But the auditor is not an agent for the supervisors and cannot do their job for them.

It is possible to envisage circumstances when the auditor's duty to the supervisors may create conflicts with his duty to his client company. Once again, if the conflict cannot be avoided it has to be managed.

It now seems generally agreed that communications between auditors and supervisors should always involve client management except in the rare instance where the interests of creditors (including depositors) or shareholders indicate that the auditors should seek direct access to supervisors or the supervisors should seek direct access to the auditors. This right of direct access, which is likely to be rarely necessary, should be common to auditors and supervisors of all supervised businesses. It also seems generally agreed that it should be governed by a framework along the lines of that suggested in the Banking Supervision White Paper (also published in December 1985) whereby:

- communications between the auditors and the supervisors are to be protected by qualified privilege, and
- guidance is provided to auditors on the circumstances in which they should consider using the right of access.

The ability of auditors to make a direct approach to the supervisors in particular circumstances, and vice versa, depends on the recognition that in such circumstances the interest of creditors and/or shareholders represent the public interest. But it is important that there should be statutory provision to ensure that auditors cannot be subject to suit from a client company or from aggrieved shareholders or creditors alleging that the company has been damaged by a communication in good faith from the auditor to the supervisors.

LITIGATION

An auditor knows that his relationship with his company client is a contractual relationship to which he is bound to bring proper skill and care. An auditor also has a duty to those who may rely on the accounts which he audits. He must be competent and he must be diligent. The auditor knows and accepts that if he fails in his professional duty, it is right that he should be open to action and that damages should be awarded if damage can be shown. And perhaps every major firm is bound to fail sometimes in its complex duty for its many thousands of clients, for which duty it employs many thousands of people. But that does not mean that the auditor is or could be the underwriter of the results of the client company or of its solvency.

Limited liability was made available to most UK companies in the last century. Limited liability for shareholders has been an essential ingredient in the growth of our capitalist, commercial society. But the auditing profession also has made a substantial contribution to the growth of that society, because the independent auditor's report has encouraged the veracity of financial statements and the honesty and credibility of the capital markets.

Until recently, auditors have been able to obtain professional indemnity insurance which has protected their firm from the risk of a catastrophic claim arising from negligence in the performance of its duty to one of its many thousands of clients. But in the last few years litigation against auditors has implied a level of liability which far exceeds cover available. The most dramatic completed litigation (though subject to appeal) is the Australian case of Fell & Starkey, where $145 million was awarded against a thirty partner firm. And in the United Kingdom there are reported to be a number of claims against auditors which substantially exceed this figure – indeed which exceed amounts which the insurance market will cover, whatever the premium.

Auditors are finding it increasingly difficult to obtain the insurance cover they consider necessary to run their business, providing an essential service to the capital markets and to the investor. Auditors are human; auditors are fallible. But it is unrealistic to look to the auditors to make good to the last penny the costs of major financial disasters. If the capital markets, the business world, need auditors,

auditors must be able to obtain protection from catastrophe stemming from their inevitable fallibility.

A press article reports a former Fell & Starkey partner, now managing partner of an important office of a major international auditing firm, as saying:

'My immediate reaction is almost to say, "Let's get out of audit!" Why bother? Why be the patsy for any company that goes down, because of a mistake in our professional judgment?'
[Business Review Weekly, 29 March 1985]

If strong and independent audit is to remain a feature of the business world, auditors cannot be the underwriters of their client companies.

INCORPORATION OF ACCOUNTING FIRMS

One solution put forward for the litigation problem is limited liability for accounting firms. Limited liability is not a solution. Nor, if it is a precursor of outside shareholders, is it desirable.

Accounting firms are already able legally to carry out non-attest, non-insolvency functions through the medium of a company – but United Kingdom law forbids us to carry out auditing services through a body corporate. On the other hand, the EEC Eighth Directive would permit bodies corporate to act as auditors, subject only to the weak proviso that a majority of the shareholders will need to be qualified auditors. Thus the EEC is already on the path which could lead to auditing firms being sold out to investors rather than remaining as partnerships of independent professionals.

The auditor as a principal

The auditor is a principal and an officer of his client company – he is not his client company's agent. His job is to express an independent opinion on information provided by others. One reasonable definition of professionalism is the ability to reach independent judgments in the midst of conflict; certainly such is the auditor's duty. In the ultimate, professional decisions must be individual – they cannot be corporate. A corporation cannot exercise judgment – '... you never expect justice from a company; it neither has a soul to lose nor a body to kick'.

Of course, the reality is that it is many years since a single, unassisted professional was able to put himself in the position where he could reach a proper judgement on the accounts of a public company. In order to reach our individual and professional judgments, we need the great structure of the major firm with all the resources of that firm, nationally and internationally, to assist us. More than that, we need a common philosophy and style of operating, not only within the partners and staff of our own office but within the partners and staff of all our offices across the world. All this is essential, but none of it denies the fundamental truth that professionalism is the exercise of individual judgment.

For this reason it is important for the quality of the judgments which we exercise, and hence the future of the profession, that every auditor, the man or woman who makes the final decision, should be a principal, not an employee, of his or her firm.

Three main reasons are being put forward to justify a change in law which would permit auditing to be carried out by a body corporate:

- the problem of partners' personal liability, relating to the current inability to obtain insurance cover which matches the claims now being made
- the difficulty of managing a partnership with several hundred partners and several thousand staff
- the need to obtain working capital otherwise than through the partners' personal wealth or bank finance.

Protection of partners' personal assets

While it may be a desirable aim to protect accountants from personal bankruptcy, this is hardly a public interest issue. The capital markets would be greatly damaged by the collapse of any major auditing firm – that is the real public interest damage which might arise from inability to obtain adequate insurance cover. And limited liability would do nothing to prevent it.

In any event, even if firms were protected by limited liability, surely the individuals involved in a specific matter, whether partners, directors or employees, would not be protected against direct action for negligence?

Management structures

The structure and management of a firm are not affected by the fact that it is a partnership. A partnership can manage itself the way it wants to, given the right partnership deed. If a firm with two hundred partners needs a 'board of directors' but the partners cannot be persuaded to agree a deed which creates one, they should look to themselves for the solution, not to Parliament.

If a firm needs a 'corporate' management structure it can create one. Many have done so.

Outside capital

Most comments on the need for new capital refer to non-attest functions – management consulting, acquisition advisory and the like. If firms need capital for these functions, they can already use corporate vehicles. It is only the attest function (and receivership and liquidation) which United Kingdom law requires to be carried out within a partnership or individual mode.

The introduction of outside capital, outside equity capital in particular, creates a new duty to shareholders and potential shareholders which could create irreconcilable conflicts with the auditors' duty to client companies and their shareholders.

If professionalism involves the exercise of independent judgment among conflicts, there comes a time when conflict becomes so difficult that you are no longer capable of being independent. Auditors already deal with conflicts between our duty and the short term interest of our firm (for instance the temptation to sign a clean audit report instead of a qualified one in order to keep the client – or the temptation to sign a qualified audit report to be safe but so bring down a viable company whose directors had made a proper judgment in preparing accounts in hard times). Today we can resolve these conflicts, we can always behave as independent professionals. The pressures of competition cannot persuade us to change this wholly proper stance. Outside capital and a duty to our own outside shareholders might.

When a company employs a firm of auditors, whom does it employ? The people who are there now, the principals who are the firm, who have grown up with it and shaped it, who are steeped in its culture and philosophy? Or a business which is owned by investor shareholders, who can sell it – or fire its people?

LLOYD'S

Nobody can discuss conflicts of interest in the United Kingdom accounting profession in 1986 without considering Lloyd's. Ian Hay Davison (formerly Deputy Chairman and Chief Executive of Lloyd's and sometime Senior Partner of Arthur Andersen in the United Kingdom) has told us that accounting firms' conflicts have played their own part in the problems at Lloyd's, for instance:

- confusion as to the identity of the accountant's client – underwriting agent or Names
- confusion of roles – accountants both keeping books and 'auditing'
- dependence on Lloyd's work – five firms, none of them household names in accounting terms, responsible for the audits of 78% of the syndicates
- clients with different interests – the same firm acting for both agents and syndicates without identifying the issues.

In a speech in Paris in April, 1985 Ian Hay Davison said:

'Under these circumstances is it any surprise that some of the auditors missed the scandals and failed to point out all the plunder that was going on. They were not charged with performing an audit to normal auditing standards and although they clearly had knowledge of some of the matters that were going on they may well not have fully appreciated their implications and they did not see it as their duty to draw the Names' attention to what was afoot. Had they been larger firms, or wiser in the affairs of the world, or perhaps more willing to ask fundamental questions then they might have exposed it quickly. But the fact is, in most cases, they did not.'

THE FUTURE

If the accounting profession has not handled all its conflicts perfectly in the past, how do we ensure that we do better in the future? What will be the future of the auditing profession as we serve the developing securities markets?

The markets are seeing the change to an instant information society. Auditors have always been in the information business. Auditing in the future is going to be very different from the past. But the conflicts are going to be no less. The auditor must first identify his client and then he can identify the conflicts and fulfil his function in the knowledge of those conflicts.

No doubt publicly traded companies and firms in the securities industry will be required to produce more information, more rapidly, with telecommunications playing an increasing part in the formal dissemination of financial information; such information must be reliable. Auditing will require new skills, but auditing is still going to be needed and it is still going to have to be independent auditing. Auditors are still going to have to make judgements amongst conflict – even though they will be using new tools and new techniques.

The accounting profession is watching the changes in the market and will make its own contributions to those changes. But the auditor is independent and must stay independent – and strong. And if the auditor is to stay independent the attest function must remain his raison d'etre; consulting must be kept as a valuable support to the attest business.

The auditor is and always has been a vital operator on the periphery of corporate finance, but the heart of corporate finance business is underwriting, financing, pricing, marketing, distribution – being part of the market. The auditor is the independent attestor to companies' accounts; he is not and cannot be in the heart of the market. The auditor is the servant of the market, not part of the market. Moreover, it is as an independent principal that he is the servant of the market. He is not the servant of his client.

The auditor must be responsible to no-one but the markets, his clients and his partners. He cannot also be responsible to his own outside shareholders, his owners. That conflict is insoluble.

Annex 1

GUIDE TO PROFESSIONAL ETHICS – INSTITUTES OF CHARTERED ACCOUNTANTS

Extracts relevant to consideration of conflicts of interest

CONSIDERATIONS OF GENERAL APPLICATION

'A member of a profession owes duties to the public, including those who retain or employ him, to the profession itself and to the other members of it. These duties may at times be contrary to his personal self-interest; the Guide is an aid to members in the identification of occasions upon which they might unwittingly fail to recognise or to fulfil any of those duties.'

'Form of guidance

'Guidance is given in the form of Fundamental Principles, Statements and Explanatory Notes.

'The *Fundamental Principles* are drawn from the duties owed by members of the profession, whether in practice or not, and from the requirements of the Charter. They are framed in broad and general terms and constitute basic advice on professional behaviour.

'They set out the overriding requirement that, as a professional man, a member must at all times perform his work objectively and impartially and free from influence by any consideration which might appear to be in conflict with this requirement. The Fundamental Principles also define a member's duties to the community. These comprise his duties to the public including those with whom he has a client relationship, or in the case of an employed member, his duties to those for whom he carries out professional work, as well as his duties to the Institute, representing the profession as a whole, and to fellow members of the profession.

'The *Statements* provide more detailed information as to what is expected of a member in certain circumstances. The fact that the Fundamental Principles are of primary importance must not, however be lost sight of, and conduct which can properly be said to be contrary to any one of them may expose a member to a complaint of misconduct, even though this act or omission does not fall specifically within the circumstances provided for by the Statements.'

'The *Explanatory Notes*, ... are indications of particular circumstances in which members could be the subject of criticism. The fact that most of these Notes relate to the Statements on Independence and Publicity indicates that these are areas in which members seem most frequently in need of advice.

'Of the first of these areas it cannot be too often emphasised that professional independence is a concept fundamental to the accountancy profession. It follows that where a member has any reasonable doubt as to the propriety of his accepting instructions he should not act.'

FUNDAMENTAL PRINCIPLES

'1. In accepting or continuing a professional assignment or occupation a member should always have regard to any factors which might reflect adversely upon his integrity and objectivity in relation to that assignment or occupation.

'2. A member should carry out his professional work with a proper regard for the technical and professional standards expected of him as a member and should not undertake or continue professional work which he is not himself competent to perform unless he obtains such advice and assistance as will enable him competently to carry out his task.

'3. A member should conduct himself with courtesy and consideration towards all with whom he comes into contact in the course of his professional work.

'4. A member should follow the ethical guidance of the Institute and in circumstances not provided for by that guidance should conduct himself in a manner consistent with the good reputation of the profession and the Institute.'

STATEMENTS

'Statement 1 – Professional independence

'Professional independence is a concept fundamental to the accountancy profession. It is essentially an attitude of mind characterised by integrity and an objective approach to professional work.

'A member in public practice should be, and be seen to be, free in each professional assignment he undertakes of any interest which might detract from objectivity. The fact that this is self-evident in the exercise of the reporting function must not obscure its relevance in respect of other professional work.

'Although a member not in public practice may be unable to be, or be seen to be, free of any interest which might conflict with a proper approach to his professional work, this does not diminish his duty of objectivity in relation to that work.

'Statement 2 – Confidentiality

'Information acquired in the course of professional work should not be disclosed except where consent has been obtained from the client, employer or other proper source, or where there is a public duty to disclose or where there is a legal or professional right or duty to disclose.

'A member acquiring information in the course of professional work should neither use nor appear to use that information for his personal advantage or for the advantage of a third party.'

'Statement 9 – Fees

'Fees should not be charged on a percentage or similar basis, save where that course is authorised by statute or is generally accepted practice for certain specialist work; nor should instructions be accepted on a contingency fee basis.'

EXPLANATORY NOTES ON STATEMENT 1

'General

'It is the duty of an accountant to present or report on information objectively. That duty is the essence of professionalism and is appropriate to all accountants in public practice, in commerce, in industry and the public service.'

'Fees

'It is undesirable that a practice should derive too great a part of its professional income from one client or group of connected clients. A practice therefore, should endeavour to ensure that the recurring fees paid by one client or group of connected clients do not exceed 15 percent of the gross fees of the practice.'

'Personal relationships

'Personal relationships can affect objectivity. There is a particular need, therefore, for a practice to ensure that its objective approach to any assignment is not endangered as a consequence of any personal relationship. By way of example, problems may arise where the same partner or senior staff member works for a number of years on the same audit or where anyone in the practice has a mutual business interest with an office or employee of a client or has an interest in a joint venture with a client. Such problems can also exist in cases of close friendship or relationship by blood or marriage or where work is being done for a company dominated by one individual.

'Financial involvement with or in the affairs of clients

'General
'Financial involvement with a client may affect objectivity. Such involvement can arise in a number of ways of which a shareholding

in a company upon which the practice is retained to report is a typical example.'

[There then follows guidance dealing with shareholdings in and borrowings from audit clients, and the like].

'Conflicts of interest

'General

'(a) In cases where conflicts of interest arise there should be a full and frank explanation to those involved, coupled with any action necessary to disengage from one or both positions, the conflicting interests of which have occasioned the difficulty. Conflicts should, so far as possible, be avoided by not accepting any appointment or assignment in which conflict seems likely to occur.

'Competing clients

'(b) As an example, a practice which advises a company upon the figures on which it bases a tender for a contract should avoid the conflict of interest which would arise if it knowingly became involved in advising a rival company tendering for the same contract.

'Clients in dispute

'(c) Another example is where a practice which is financial adviser to a company also deals with the personal affairs of its directors and there is a dispute between the company and one of those directors. In such a case a practice should select which of its clients it is to advise. It should not advise both and it may well be preferable that it advises neither although it may, if asked by both clients, put forward proposals for settling the dispute. Similar considerations apply in the case of a partnership dispute.

'Provision of other services to audit clients

'Whilst it is right that members should provide, for audit clients, other services beyond performing the audit, nevertheless care must be taken not to perform executive functions or to make executive decisions. These are the duties of management ... In particular members should beware lest, in providing such services they drift into a situation in which they step across the border-line of what is proper.'

[There is also guidance preventing acceptance of appointment as liquidator of a company to which a partner has been receiver or as receiver (or liquidator in an insolvent liquidation) of a company with which the firm has had a previous continuing professional relationship].

Annex 2

EXTRACTS FROM RULES AND GUIDANCE ON INDEPENDENCE FOR THE MANAGEMENT GROUP OF PEAT MARWICK UNITED KINGDOM

'Introduction

'It should be emphasised that whilst guidance can be given, the most important standard by which to judge independence is the individual's professional integrity.

'Restrictions are applied to partners and staff in relation, inter alia, to investment in client companies and the confidentiality of clients' affairs and those of the Firm, which are embodied in a declaration signed on joining the Firm.

'It is a fundamental principle that every member of the management group shall remain completely independent of clients for whom the firm is engaged to express an opinion on financial statements.

'Prohibited securities

'Members of the management group should not have or become committed to acquire, directly or indirectly, any financial interest in:

(i) a publicly-traded company which is an audit client of any Peat Marwick firm and any of its related companies which are themselves publicly traded, or

(ii) a publicly-traded company which is not an audit client of any Peat Marwick firm but for which a material segment of the group [defined as 10% in terms of net assets, profit or turnover] is audited by any Peat Marwick firm, or

(iii) a publicly-traded company with which the UK Firm has a continuing close involvement in an advisory capacity, or

(iv) any company registered with the US Securities and Exchange Commission which is not an audit client of any Peat Marwick firm but for which a non-material segment is audited by the UK Firm, or

(v) any other audit client of the UK Firm.

'In this context "directly or indirectly" includes the member's close family (i.e. spouse, dependent children, and any other relatives who are either living permanently in the member's household, or who are being given financial support of a substantial nature) trusts, investment clubs and personal holding companies which provide benefit by way of income or residual interest to the member of his family. It does not include an interest as a beneficiary of a trust where the member of the management group is not a trustee.'

The rules continue to deal with the following (inter alia):

- to explain that the Firm publishes annually an International Register of Prohibited Securities
- to forbid participation in a business expansion fund which is or whose management company is an audit client and to allow investment in other funds provided thay have a facility to ensure that no investment in Peat Marwick is allocated to a Peat Marwick participant
- to draw attention to the prohibition on dealing on insider information, whether or not in relation to audit clients
- to deal with situations where Peat Marwick people inadvertently become owners of prohibited securities
- to forbid acceptance of executorships and trusteeships unless the trust prohibits investment in prohibited securities
- to prevent a Peat Marwick person from joining a Lloyds syndicate which is or is managed by an audit client etc.
- to prohibit commercial relationships with clients which could impair independence
- to forbid acceptance of directorships.

The management group consists of the Firm's partners and managers. The rules for other staff are similar except that the prohibition on investment extends only to audit clients of which the employee's office audits a material segment, rather than to audit clients of any office in the world.

INDEPENDENCE DECLARATION

Each partner or staff member has to sign a declaration as of 31st March in each year. For example, that for management group staff is as follows:

'1. I confirm I have read and will observe the Firm's "Rules and Guidance on Independence-Management Group".

'2. I undertake to comply with the above and agree that the continuance of my employment by the Firm is dependent on my strict compliance therewith.

'3 I agree at all times during my employment and afterwards to keep secret the affairs of the firm and its clients.

'4. I have reviewed the securities held by myself and my close family in conjunction with the current International Register of Prohibited Securities and confirm that, subject to the exceptions noted below, neither I nor any member of my close family holds or is committed to acquire any security which is prohibited or restricted.

'5. I confirm that neither I nor my spouse nor my close family:

  (i) own shares in a Lloyd's members agency,

 (ii) own shares in a Lloyd's managing agency,

(iii) are underwriting members of Lloyd's.

'6. I confirm that neither I nor my spouse have any investments in a Business Expansion fund which is an audit client or whose management company is an audit client or in an investment of any other fund where that investment is a Peat Marwick prohibited company.'

FINANCIAL CONGLOMERATES AND CONFLICTS OF INTEREST

Philip R. Wood

1 INTRODUCTION

In speaking of the standard of conduct which the courts require from a person in a fiduciary position, Cardozo CJ observed in *Meinhard* v. *Salmon*[1]:

> 'Many forms of conduct permissible in a work-a-day world for those acting at arm's length are forbidden to those bound by fiduciary ties. A trustee is held to something stricter than the morals of the market place. Not honesty alone, but the punctilio of an honour the most sensitive, is then the standard of behaviour. As to this there has developed a tradition that is unbending and inveterate. Uncompromising rigidity has been the attitude of courts of equity when petitioned to undermine the rule of undivided loyalty by the "disintegrating erosion" of particular exceptions.'

If one were to take this standard as applying to the investment banking and dealing activities of the London financial conglomerate, it would be impossible to do business.

Of course the presence of conflicts of interest in securities dealing and banking has always been there. But the new linking-up of, on the one side, commercial and merchant banking with, on the other, brokers and dealers in securities, leads to a huge increase in the potential conflicts of interest.

This paper is intended as a background to the new financial services legislation and the rules to be made thereunder which, at the time of writing, had not been settled.

2 CONFLICTING CAPACITIES

Examples of capacities

A financial conglomerate may act in numerous capacities. It may be:

1. 249 NY 458 (1928) at 464.

- a banker financing the issuer of securities and owing the issuer duties of confidence and care
- a dealer in securities for its own account
- an investment adviser, owing duties to its client
- a market-maker dealing on its own account
- a manager of unit trusts and pension funds, owing duties to a floating class of beneficiaries
- an investment manager of discretionary accounts owing duties to a specific client
- a trustee of will trusts, owing duties to the beneficiaries of the estate
- a corporate financial adviser, owing duties to the company
- a trustee of debt or convertible issues, owing duties to the bond-holders
- an agent bank, owing duties to a syndicate of banks.

Examples of conflicts

The possibilities of conflicts of interest are legion.

As regards the underwriting arm, the underwriter may be long on an issue, and so be tempted to dump the long position in captive discretionary accounts. If the proceeds of the issue are to be used to pay back a parent bank private loan, there may be a temptation to cut corners on the prospectus and on promotion.

As regards the fund management arm, there may be pressure from the corporate finance arm to support clients by buying its securities or voting managed holdings in a particular way. There may be a temptation of the broking or market-making arm to dump securities in the funds. There may be pressure from the broking arm to generate commissions by as many transactions as possible.

As regards the broking arm, the broker may be tempted to improve profits by buying-in ordered securities and selling them on. His advice may be distorted by overriders and lose its independence. He may be tempted to use clients' uninvested balances to finance the firm, and delay in executing transactions or paying out to the customer. He may be led into dual agencies (acting for both sides) by a desire to match deals in order to obtain two commissions.

As regards the banking arm, the corporate finance arm may know of a default which would be very material to the banking arm acting as a syndicate agent. The banking arm would be seriously compromised where it is the banker to a target while the corporate finance arm is advising the predator.

Generally there is a potential flow of confidential and price-sensitive information about securities between broking, investment, banking and trustee arms, and all manner of pressures to improve the return on assets.

3 THE LAW AND FIDUCIARIES

No fixed rules

There are no fixed rules about conflicts of interest. Every conflict has to be examined according to the circumstances. The test is whether the fiduciary's discretions and powers on behalf of his principal might be polluted by his personal interest or by a divided loyalty. The rule is based on the hallowed orison 'lead us not into temptation.' The key is the degree of risk that the fiduciary's mind will be poisoned.

One can hardly over-emphasise the overriding importance of the particular facts. In *Re Coomber*[2] Fletcher Moulton LJ said[3]:

'It is said that the son was the manager of the stores and therefore was in a fiduciary relationship to his mother. This illustrates in a most striking form the danger of trusting to verbal formulae. Fiduciary relations are of many different types; they extend from the relation of myself to an errand boy who is bound to bring me back my change up to the most intimate and confidential relations which can possibly exist between one party and another where the one is wholly in the hands of the other because of his infinite trust in him. All these are cases of fiduciary relations, and the Courts have again and again, in cases where there has been a fiduciary relation, interfered and set aside acts which, between persons in a wholly independent position, would have been perfectly valid. Thereupon in some minds there arises the idea that if there is any fiduciary relation whatever any of these types of interference is warranted by it. They conclude that every kind of fiduciary relation justifies every kind of interference. Of course that is absurd. The nature of the fiduciary relation must be such that it justifies the interference. There is no class of case in which one ought more carefully to bear in mind the facts of the case, when one reads the judgment of the Court on those facts, than cases which relate to fiduciary and confidential relations and the action of the Court with regard to them.'

2. [1911] 1 Ch 723.
3. At 728.

Self-dealing and secret profits

However, whilst particular facts control, the law has erected two rules into principles of virtually universal application. These are:

(1) The prohibition against undisclosed *self-dealing*. An agent cannot secretly sell his own property to his principal or secretly buy his principal's property for himself. In *Rothschild* v. *Brookman*[4] a purchase of a client's stock by a broker was set aside. In *Lucifero* v. *Castel*[5] an agent was instructed to buy a yacht; he bought one himself and resold it to his principal at a considerable mark-up. The agent could recover only what he paid for the yacht. In *Regier* v. *Campbell-Stuart*[6] the agent gave the pretended purchase price to the principal. The principal could recover the undisclosed excess profit. In *Nicholson* v. *Mansfield*[7] the broker charged a commission plus a mark-up without disclosing this. Held: the client could repudiate.

It is immaterial that the transaction is fair e.g. the price at which the agent traded was the market price.[8]

(2) The prohibition against *secret profits*. A secret profit is a surreptitious financial advantage obtained by the agent by the use of his position. It includes a secret mark-up. In *De Bussche* v. *Alt*[9] an agent was instructed to sell a ship at a specified price. He could not find a buyer at that price. So he bought the ship himself at that price. Later he sold it to X at a higher price. Held: breach of duty. It is irrelevant that there is no corruption or that the agent was not influenced by the profit or bribe. A discount, such as a volume discount, not passed on to the principal, falls into the same category of secret profits.[10] The classic case of *Boardman* v. *Phipps*[11] illustrates how uncompromisingly the law has set its face against the use by a fiduciary of his position to gain an advantage. Foreign exchange gains made by the agent will belong to the principal.[12] But there is no objection if the profit is not

---

4. (1831) 2 Dow & Cl 188.
5. (1887) 3 TLR 371.
6. [1936] Ch 766.
7. (1901) 17 TLR 259.
8. *Gillett* v. *Peppercorne* (1840) 3 Beav 78; *Aberdeen Railway* v. *Blaikie Bros* (1854) 1 Macq 461; *Armstrong* v. *Jackson* [1917] 2 KB 822.
9. (1878) 8 Ch D 286.
10. See *Turnbull* v. *Garden* (1869) 20 LT 218.
11. [1967] 2 AC 46.
12. *Diplock* v. *Blackburn* (1811) 3 Camp 43.

secret.[13] Reasonable but undisclosed charges for transfer services carried out have been allowed.[14]

Part of the reason for the rigidity of the prohibitions against self-dealing and secret profits is deterrence and expedience. Otherwise it would be too easy for the agent to evade the fiduciary obligation and too difficult for the beneficiary to show that the agent's powers were poisoned by the conflict of interest. The rules are sometimes punitive, but the answer of the law is that the agent always has the ability to disclose the position and obtain his principal's consent.

Likelihood of conflict

Is the rule infringed if conflict is merely possible or must it be probable?

The formulation of the doctrine by Lord Cranworth LC in *Aberdeen Railway Co v. Blaikie Bros*[15] is probably too wide. He says

'It is a rule of universal application that no-one having such duties to discharge shall be allowed to enter into an engagement in which he has, or can have, a personal interest conflicting, or *which possibly may conflict* with the interests of those whom he is bound to protect' (emphasis added).

In *Industrial Development Consultants v. Cooley*[16] Roskill J said:[17]

'The phrase "possibly may conflict" requires consideration. In my view it means that the reasonable man looking at the relevant facts and circumstances of the particular case would think that there was a real sensible possibility of conflict; not that you could imagine some situation arising which might, in some conceivable possibility in events not contemplated as real sensible possibilties by any reasonable person, result in conflict.'

Firms as fiduciaries

A firm acting in an agency or advisory capacity will generally be a fiduciary and subject to the duty of economic loyalty. Where a firm

13. See for example *Hippisley v. Knee* [1905] 1 KB 1.
14. See *Stubbs v. Slater* [1910] 1 Ch 632.
15. (1854) 1 Macq 461 at 471, HL.
16. [1972] 2 All ER 162.
17. At 172.

is strictly acting as a known counterparty then it may not be a fiduciary. On the other hand, where a firm has habitually been acting as an agent for a client, the law has not permitted the agent to switch roles and abruptly treat himself as a counterparty and thereby evade the burdens of fiduciary duty – at least not without the informed consent of the client. Once a fiduciary always a fiduciary, unless the break is clear and the ascendancy has gone.

Whether an underwriter is a fiduciary depends on the role he plays in managing the issue.

Discretions

The degree of loyalty should depend in part upon the degree of discretion vested in the firm, e.g. the firm's power to affect the financial position of the client. Thus if a firm is instructed to buy a particular security at a particular price, the dangers of conflict are inevitably lessened, although not removed altogether. In the decision of the Ontario Court of Appeal in *Deacon* v. *Varga*[18] the court held that:

'the primary duty of an agent [in this case a stockbroker] is to carry out the instructions of his principal . . . the duty of disclosure arises where there is a conflict of interest between the principal and agent or where the principal had imposed such a term in the agency agreement. If the principal authorises his agent to act imprudently or he acts upon his own decision without relying on his agent's advice then he really cannot complain about any resulting loss.'

Professionals

The sophistication and financial resilience of the client should be relevant. Commonsense indicates that a broker dealing with the financial director of a large public company should have a lesser responsibility than where he is investing the life savings of a widow in Hastings: he has less power and there is less reliance. There is a general trend of the law in other fields to distinguish between the businessman and the layman, but it would be wrong to assume that the conflicts rules do not apply to dealings with professionals, and indeed many of the cases concern commercial transactions between

18. (1973) 30 DLR (3a) 653.

businessmen. The distinction between the professional and non-professional investor is likely to be a leading feature of the scope of conduct of business rules and is fundamental in other areas of securities regulation e.g. the issue of prospectuses. Unhappily application of the double standard to conflicts is unclear and one is left to reason it out in the light of sensible principle.

Intensity of conflict

The intensity of the potential conflict is relevant. For example where a bank, which is a private lender to an issuer of bonds, acts as trustee of a bond issue by that issuer, the potentiality for conflict is not usually as intense as a case where the trustee is controlled by the issuer. In the latter case it would be out of the question for the bank to act as trustee, but not perhaps in the former case.

Similarly the potential conflict for a broker who is also a market-maker is not as intense as the potential conflict between underwriting and fund management. Of course a broker/market-maker may have a monopoly trading position and by virtue of his knowledge of the book he can, by moving the price of his specialities up and down, guarantee himself profits in both his broker and dealer functions. As the SEC has found, it is by no means easy to curb abuses in this area by specific rule-making.

Divided loyalty

Conflicts of interest are not limited to the conflict between the duty to a client and the firm's personal interest. There is another important case of conflict, namely that of divided loyalty or acting for both sides.[20] Here the firm has conflicting duties to two masters so that whatever the fiduciary does he is liable to one or the other. An example is the duty of the corporate finance arm to an issuer and the duty of the investment advisory arm to a client. An acute difficulty can arise where the corporate finance arm has price-sensitive information which the investment advisory arm must exclude from its tip sheets, with the result that the advisory arm cannot properly give sound advice. Another example of the divided loyalty is the put-through or dual agency. In Australia a custom of matching buy and sell transactions has been held reasonable.[21]

20. See for example *Fullwood* v. *Hurley* [1928] 1 KB 498; *Anglo-African Merchants Ltd* v. *Bayley* [1969] 2 All ER 241 *North & South Trust Co* v. *Berkeley* [1971] 1 All ER 980.
21. *Jones* v. *Canavan* (1972) 2 NSWLR 236.

4 REMEDIES OF INJURED CLIENT

Examples of remedies

Where a firm acts in conflict of interest, the law and the regulators can impose a wide array of sanctions, some of them punitive. The availability of the particular remedy depends on the circumstance.

The client may be able to remove the agent, e.g. terminate an investment management contract or remove a bond trustee.

The client may be able to obtain an injunction against the agent acting in breach of duty. This could be potentially important for bids.

The client may be able to rescind the contract, subject to the usual rules concerning laches and express or implied affirmation of the transaction.

The client may be able to insist that the firm disgorges any secret profit or gain and returns any commission. The firm may have to disgorge the profit made on a resale of securities bought from the client by the agent or the profit on an on-sale of securities bought in by the agent.[22] A bond trustee may be obliged to disgorge a private loan recovered by the bond trustee ahead of bondholders.

The client may be able to claim compensation for any loss suffered. The proposed legislation contains an express right of damages for breach of the various code regulations to be observed by members of the self-regulatory organisations. The legislation also contemplates that action for compensation may be officially initiated as a counter to client inertia, client inexperience or client impecuniousness.

A fiduciary is in principle more·vulnerable to negligence proceedings on the ground that the conflict of interest may be characterised as bad faith, weakening exculpation clauses or putting the fiduciary on extra proof of diligence.[23] This affects, for example, investment management contracts, corporate finance advice and the monitoring duties of bond trustees.

The firm may be subject to the removal of its dealing licence. This

---

22. *Tyrrell* v. *Bank of London* (1862) 10 HL Cas 26; contrast *Jacobus Marler Estates Ltd* v. *Marler* (1913) 85 LJPC 167 where it was held that only rescission or damages (if any) are available where the agent sells to his principal property already held by him, but commission is in any event not chargeable.
23. See *Mutual Life & Citizens Assurance Co* v. *Evatt* [1977] 1 All ER 150; *Dabney* v. *Chase National Bank*, 346 US 863 (1953).

is too draconian to be used much and may be regarded as primarily a moraliser and the ultimate threat.

The firm may be subjected to public censure and administrative fines.

In serious cases the firm may be subject to criminal penalties. The criminal penalties do not apply merely to those specific crimes which have been outlawed by securities regulation e.g. insider trading. The high foreground of the law continues to be held by the generalised crimes such as conspiracy and obtaining a pecuniary advantage by deception. This has long been the case. The following have all been held to be criminal frauds: the deliberate concealment of the financial state of the issuer of securities; the sale of securities to a client concealing that they were securities originally held by the agent; the purchase of securities and their subsequent on-sale to the customer at a deliberately concealed profit; the taking of secret commissions. See also the Prevention of Corruption Acts, 1906/16.

A wronged beneficiary has various procedural advantages: the onus of proof may shift to the firm; time does not run in certain cases; a fiduciary may not set off profits and losses on two unauthorised transactions; the beneficiary has a more favourable interest rule; the beneficiary may be able to trace.

Weakness of remedies

These remedies suffer the usual weaknesses. One is client inertia. Another is the concealment of wrong-doing. Transaction tapes may help the audit trail but the problem of recording transactions in the OTC and outside markets prevails. Monitoring bodies cannot check everything. Nor are they likely to have the resources to follow up every alleged abuse.

At the end of the day reliance must be placed on the integrity of the market. This can only work if practitioners are sensitive to the rigour of the law.

Impact of competition

It has been argued that the forces of competition will counter to a large extent the dangers of conflicts of interest. No doubt competition will force out the habitual churners. On the other hand once the private club has gone and its chivalric codes of courtesy – which despite some shocking exceptions were generally honoured – have been effaced, there must be a risk that the pressure to win business will increase the temptation to indulge in smart practices.

5 CONDUCT OF BUSINESS RULES AND THE LAW

Double layer of law

Conduct of business rules made under the financial services legislation will set out particular obligations of financial conglomerates. But it will not be enough merely to observe the letter of the code. The general law is not excluded. There is therefore a double layer of law: the codes themselves and, behind these, the brooding presence of the law relating to fiduciaries.

Chinese walls

A Chinese wall is a fence around each of the potentially conflicting departments so that information and interests in one department are not known to the other. The fence must establish a complete operational and physical separation to prevent flows of information between the conflicting departments.

In this context it may be noted that the veil of incorporation is not in itself effective as a Chinese wall. Thus case law has demonstrated that an agent cannot avoid the self-dealing prohibition by selling his principal's property to a company controlled by him.[24] It is plain that the fence is incomplete if the two corporations have the same personnel or have different personnel who act in accordance with the interests of the group as a whole.

There is nothing new about the Chinese wall concept. The principle of divided knowledge has been sanctioned from early days: see the dangerous dog cases (where one servant knew the dog was a biter but the other did not), and the case involving co-trustees and co-directors (where only one of them is guilty of a breach of duty). But opposed to these cases are the decisions imputing the knowledge of an agent to his principal, and the knowledge of an employee to his employer. Hence specific legislative sanction is needed. Indeed legislative recognition has recently been given to Chinese walls in Australia, the US and the UK in certain cases.

Some disadvantages of the Chinese wall are as follows:

– the wall inhibits an advantage of integration, such as pooled expertise and pooled resources. There is more expense. It must however be remembered that one of the main aims of integration is financial muscle, and one of its chief motives the market require-

---

24. *Salomons* v. *Pender* (1865) 3 H & C 639.

ment for the development of larger groups capable of multiple capacity

- the wall may inhibit the identification of acute conflicts in time, especially in takeovers
- senior executives in charge of monitoring (the compliance officers) must be excluded from certain decision-making or communicating conflicts to other executives. This may strike at the concept of collective board responsibility and involve a split of management control
- the wall is particularly thin in small firms
- the wall might crumble before the pressures of self-interest
- stop lists may feed rumours and confirm hunches. A firm with numerous clients may have an overlong restricted list so that it is less competitive
- the wall is overflown if information is publicly available. For example if the investment management arm learns from the newspapers that the corporate finance arm is engaged in a contested bid, the conglomerate may tend to act in a concerted fashion.

Disclosure

The cornerstone of the policy of mitigating conflicts of interest is disclosure. This is effectively the only way to contract out. There will be a general code obligation to disclose all material interests.

The basic rule enunciated in the cases is of full disclosure and consent. It was said in a leading case that the beneficiary can relax the duty provided he 'fully understands not only what he is doing but also what his legal rights are and that he is in part surrendering them.'[25]

This strict rule leads to a number of problems.

First, what is a *material* interest? This involves the exercise of judgment with only general guidance from the cases and patchy guidance from the rule-book for the more obvious situations.

Secondly, is a general disclosure enough and in what circumstances? The cases suggest that it is not enough for a fiduciary merely to disclose that he has an interest.[26] It is not enough for a fiduciary to make statements that would put his principal on enquiry.[27] On the other hand statute has sanctioned general disclosure in certain circumstances e.g. disclosure at directors' meetings

25. *Boulting* v. *ACTT* [1963] 1 All ER 716, CA, at p. 729.
26. *Alexander* v. *Automatic Telephone Co* [1900] 2 Ch 56.
27. *Dunne* v. *English* (1874) LR 18 Eq 524.

of a personal interest by a director. *Ellis & Co* v. *Watsham*[28] exemplifies a commonsense attitude to sufficient disclosure. Here the stockbrokers sent the client two contract notes on which were the words 'bought of ourselves as principals'. No commission was charged. The client paid part of the price, the balance being carried over. It is held that the stockbrokers had made sufficiently full and accurate disclosure to the client that they were selling as principals and that the client, with full knowledge, gave his assent to the position.

Practice is often at variance with a strict doctrine of specific disclosure. Thus trust deeds for bond issues and agency clauses in syndicated loan agreements contain general disclosure clauses which are by no means particular or specific.

Specific disclosure will often be impracticable. How can a financial conglomerate disclose in specific detail its multiple interests which might be material? How can a bank acting as bond trustee disclose details of its private loans to an issuer?

Plainly distinctions have to be made. Much depends on the intensity of the conflict. Much depends on what has to be disclosed.

Having regard to the prohibition on self-dealing, it is axiomatic that disclosure of capacity – whether agent or principal – is obligatory. But even from this rule there may need to be some exceptions e.g. for stabilisation, odd-lots and bona fide arbitrage transactions.

Stabilisation incidentally is a good example of an activity which breaks practically every rule in the compliance manual (market-rigging, insider trading, short selling etc.) but is nevertheless considered to be a legitimate operation in the interests of an orderly primary distribution. Many modern securities codes e.g. in the United States, Japan, Canada, Australia and, one hopes, the United Kingdom feel obliged to exempt bona fide stabilisation from the operation of the usual prohibitions.

A further example is block positioning. Institutions often trade in large blocks which put special strains on exchange market making mechanisms. If a firm has an institutional customer which wishes to sell 100,000 shares of a particular security but can only find buyers for 80,000, the firm may wish to position the remaining 20,000 shares and sell them off over a period of time as the market can absorb them. This may offend the self dealing rule. On the other hand the positioning ought to be recognised as a legitimate exception.

A particularly sensitive question is the degree of disclosure of mark-ups.

Apart from these familiar examples, there is the question of dis-

28. (1923) 1 55 LT Jo 363.

closure of long positions by a firm, especially if an investment is not dealt in on a recognised exchange. There is the question of disclosure of collateral held by a broker or its affiliates over the securities in question.

A third problem is whether a general consent given in advance as opposed to a specific consent on each occasion will suffice. The objection to a prior general consent is that the client is being asked in advance to waive a protection without knowing in detail exactly what he is consenting to do.

A fourth problem is that Chinese walls may prevent acute conflicts from being identified until too late.

A fifth problem is the objection to the disclosure of privileged or confidential information, particularly for commercial/merchant investment banks. Confidentiality collides with disclosure.

Finally, the unsophisticated investor may take the disclosure as itself a sign of perfect integrity. But a consequence of disclosure may be: 'I have told you about my temptations. I can now yield to them.'

Shingle theory

Basic to any conduct of business rules is that the dealer must have an adequately informed basis for his recommendations. The shingle theory holds that a dealer who turns out a shingle as a dealer in securities must conform to the standards of a professional expert. In a US administrative action in 1977, a US securities firm was fined US$1.6m damages and sanctions were imposed on 28 salesmen for alleged unsubstantiated recommendations of the stock of an electronics company.

The shingle theory is no more than an elaboration of a general protection available at law encompassed in the general duty of an agent to act in the best interest of his principal.

Scalping

One may at this point mention scalping. Scalping occurs where an adviser, for example a financial journalist, recommends a security he has secretly bought with a view to selling the paper when consumers buy on the faith of his recommendation. Scalping has been held to be a fraud in the United States.[29] In certain circumstances the practice may be treated as a fraud in England. Investment advisers should

29. SEC v. *Capital Gains Research Bureau* 375 US 180 (1963); *Zwieg* v. *Hearst Corporation* 594 F 2d 1261 (9th Cir 1979).

consider the risk of scalping as regard tip sheets where the advising firm itself holds the securities it recommends.

Churning

Conduct of business rules attack a variety of remuneration-related abuses.

One example is churning. This term applies to excessive transactions to generate as much commission as possible and has been held a fraud in the United States. The traditional code protection is that transactions must not be excessive in size or frequency having regard to the investment objectives, financial situation and needs of the client.

Churning is particularly difficult to monitor, even where reports must be made to the regulatory agency of the firm's earnings on a particular account. Churning should in any event be caught by the general duty of economic loyalty owed by an agent.

Churning also includes the classic market-rigging exercise of repeated artificial and screen-visible transactions to force up the price.[30]

Excessive charging

Excessive charging has come in for judicial and regulatory attention.[31] This abuse may, in a era of free commissions, be controlled by the forces of competition.

Precise regulation has obstacles. For example it cannot always be the rule that a firm must charge the minimum. It would be unreasonable to expect an investment manager always to obtain the lowest fee and to act as a cut-rate commission merchant. He should be able to take into account his other service to the client e.g. research. Certainly US experience has found this relaxation to be necessary.

One key to the control of remuneration abuses is the disclosure of mark-ups.

Suitability rule

This rule holds that the transaction must be suitable to the client's financial situation so far as it can be ascertained. The rule is – 'know thy customer'. The scope of permissible conflicts must be influenced in appropriate cases by the status of the client. Thus it is essential

30. See *Norris & Hirshberg* v. *SEC*, 177 F 21 288 (DC Cir 1949).
31. See *Charles Hughes & Co* v. *SEC*, 139 F 2d 434 (2d Cir 1943).

for the firm to have adequate knowledge of its customer and his financial position. A client's personal circumstances may change.

Best execution rule

This rule holds that the firm must obtain the best possible price. In the case of screen deals this should not be difficult. But in the case of illiquid or unquoted securities, price checks in the market are necessary. The rule is particularly important where a dealer sells as principal. The firm as seller must give at least as good a deal as if the firm had bought from another counterparty in the market.

Priority rule

The rule here is that the client's order must come first.

If a client orders a sale of a block of securities, the price may fall. So the broker or his affiliates or employees may be tempted to sell their stock before completing the client sale.

If the client orders a purchase, the price may go up: the broker and his associates may be tempted to buy first.

Appropriation of bargains

Where a dealer buys a line of stock with a view to distributing them amongst clients, the rule holds that the broker must appropriate immediately. There might otherwise be a temptation to appropriate to the clients if the securities go down and to the firm if they go up.

Information to client

As observed above, disclosure is the cornerstone of the defence against conflicts of interest.

Conduct of business rules envisage elaborate customer agreements dealing with the services to be performed, with investment guidelines, and with remuneration, and will contain special rules about termination and the client's requirements as regards gearing.

This necessitates much paper (not altogether ameliorated by data equipment) and time stamping e.g. recording the timing of instructions, the timing of the decision to invest and the timing of execution, in order to facilitate a proper audit.

Practical considerations emphasise the special importance of an efficient clearing and transfer system through a clearing agent and depository.

Contract notes will need to disclose capacity and mark-ups. The familiar question of whether a post-contract disclosure is adequate may arise on occasion.

Limitations of conduct of business rules

Conduct of business rules particularise the general. Their chief limitation is that the rule-book cannot substitute black-letter law for the exercise of judgment in all cases, nor can the rule-book cover all circumstances. Nevertheless, specific codes are essential. Judicial recognition will depend on how closely they reflect the general law. Plentiful decisions illustrate the proposition that the courts will not uphold market customs which are unreasonable, e.g. a custom which allows self-dealing.[32]

6 EXTRATERRITORIALITY

Securities regulation is local. But securities trading is international. It is inevitable therefore that there may be a collision between high and low regulated states.

The low regulated states are not to be identified solely with island republics and colonies. In fact the most important low regulated states are situated in Europe. For historical reasons, Germany, Switzerland and (at least until recently) the Netherlands have had no securities regulation at all in the traditional common law sense – although there have been other controls exercised either through stock exchange self-regulation or through central bank controls of the currency and hence of issues. These countries will argue that they have never needed the ant-like securities regulation espoused by the common law states. Perhaps they are right and perhaps the reason that a formal structure was not required was – and to some extent still is – that the securities market and stock exchanges were monopolised by a few universal banks who were the equivalent of the SEC in terms of practical function. Nevertheless there must be a danger that an officer in a bank branch in a low regulated state will communicate a transaction to a high regulated state without realising that he is doing wrong.

The US courts, aided by the American Law Institute in its Restatement, have been particularly energetic in fertilising guidelines for prescriptive jurisdiction, primarily in the anti-trust area but with significant case law in the area of securities regulation. The most

32. *Robinson* v. *Millett* (1875) LR 7 HL 802.

controversial question is whether a regulating state can punish a foreign offender on the basis that the foreign misconduct has adverse consequences within the regulating estate although no actual proscribed act takes place in the regulated state – the 'results' doctrine. It would not be right to regard extraterritoriality or the export of securities regulation as a purely US phenomenon. The English long-arm jurisdictional rules for torts (including breach of statutory duty) are wide. Further the English courts have built up their own concepts of prescriptive jurisdiction. Curiously some of the leading cases concern pornographic material.

7 TRUSTEES OF BOND ISSUES

Introduction

Trustees are probably held to a higher standard than ordinary agents. There are two approaches

(a) a statute sets out deemed conflicts which disqualify the trustee from acting under a regulated trust deed for non-exempt debt issues to the public. This is the approach in the US, Australia and Singapore. The deemed conflicts are non-exclusive.

(b) the rule of law does not identify conflicts but proscribes conflicts generally. This is the approach in England, Luxembourg and France.

Examples of conflicts

Set out below are some examples of conflicting capacities.

There are *cross-shareholdings* or *cross-directorships*. It should be out of the question for a company to act as a trustee for an issue by its subsidiary. The size of the shareholding which might affect the trustee's purity will depend on the facts. US statute puts the threshold at 20%, France at 10% and Singapore at 5% – a bewildering range.

The trustee *guarantees* the issue. Here the trustee is both prosecution and defence.

The trustee is a *trustee of two issues* of the same issuer in which case both classes of bondholders might be competing for the same assets. English trustees are usually willing to act on issues of the same class (e.g. two unsecured bond issues). Whether they can act if issues are of a differing class (e.g. one secured and the other unsecured) depends on an analysis of the circumstances. Thus the possibility of conflict is perhaps not serious where one issue is senior and the other subordinated, on account of the limited action which the junior holders can take to protect themselves against the senior holders.

The trustee is also a *private lender* to the issuer, e.g. where the trustee is a bank. The bank might be tempted to secure the payment of its own loan first, to call for private security or to insist on building up set-offs. The bank might be privy to information which is protected by banker's confidentiality but which is highly pertinent to the bondholders. There might be a temptation not to notify defaults, or an inclination to advance more private money to avert a default, or not to accelerate the bonds if the acceleration might prejudice the recoverability of the private loan. Experience has shown that a bank lender who is also a trustee has severely restricted freedom of action as lender in the event of default, and is exposed to bondholder action if holders go unpaid.

The trustee has a *trustee investment department* which invests securities for customers under discretionary accounts or holds securities under will trusts. The interests of the trustee as a shareholder for the account of its customers and its duties to the bondholders could be in conflict. This is a case of divided loyalty as opposed to conflicting personal interest.

The trustee acts as *financial adviser* to an issuer. The advice may be in conflict with the best interests of the bondholders. Alternatively the corporate finance department may come to know of a default in circumstances imposing a duty of confidentiality.

A member of the same group as the trustee has one of the above relationships with the issuer. The trustee's wish to protect its fellow company may conflict with its duties to bondholders.

Resignation as a remedy

Of course, if a conflict actually surfaces, the trustee could resign, but this apparent escape is, in practice, limited, because the resignation itself may tend to create alarm, the bondholders lose an informed trustee when they need him most, and experience has shown that some trustees are reluctant to resign when they are in this privileged position until it is too late.

English position

In England there are no *statutory* rules regarding conflicts of interest of a trustee. This is partly because of the almost penal attitude of the English courts to fiduciary conflicts, and because banks desisted from acting as trustees after some scathing judicial criticism of conflicting roles and of clauses permitting the trustee to act despite a conflict.[33] Hence, conflicts were less common perhaps than in the US during the Depression days. However, the English courts have been emphatic that the trustee must not put himself in a position where his duty and his interest conflict. Whilst the rules have been developed in relation to private trusts (e.g. a trustee cannot receive payment for his services unless specifically allowed, or purchase the trust property or set himself up in competition with a business included in the trust) the general principles undoubtedly apply to business trusts.

The Stock Exchange rules for London listings prescribe that the trustee 'must have no interest in or relation to the company which might conflict with the position of trustee'. The rule refrains from elaboration.

United States

In the United States the Trust Indenture Act of 1939 has intervened to prevent a trustee of a regulated indenture from acting if there is a material conflict of interest. The Act, in a busy section 310(b), sets out nine interests which are deemed to be conflicting, e.g. cross-control, being a trustee under more than one indenture for the same obligor (except under certain conditions), being an underwriter of the securities, or if 20% or more of the trustee's voting shares are owned by the obligor and its directors or officers combined (or more than 10% owned by one such person). Only very limited interlocking of boards of directors is allowed. It is clear however that the Act does not override the common law responsibilties of a trustee so that these survive parallel to the 1939 Act.[34]

Interestingly enough, the Act does not prohibit a trustee from also being a private lender to or other creditor of the obligor. There is merely a limited protection imposing a sharing of receipts when a default is looming. Section 311(a) of the Act provides that if the trustee becomes a creditor of the obligor within four months prior or subsequent to uncured defaults then the trustee must in effect hold in a separate account for the benefit of investors amounts equal to the reductions of the private claims and property received by the trustee against those claims. However, the section is not all powerful

33. *Re Dorman Long & Co Ltd* [1934] 1 Ch D, 953.
34. *Morris* v. *Cantor*, 390 F. Supp 817 (SDNY 1975).

since it excludes some creditor claims of the trustee in its private capacity and furthermore the four-month rule is rather short in the context of many defaults. On the other hand, as will be seen, case law has intervened to cause a trustee to disgorge private moneys received even outside the four-month period.

Some of the US cases on conflicts of interest are of interest:

Dabney v. *Chase National Bank of the City of New York.*[35] An action was brought against the trustee in order to restore loan payments which the trustee had received eight years prior to the declaration of bankruptcy of the obligor, on the basis that the loan was made when the trustee had knowledge of the borrower's insolvency. The loan had been made and repaid during the trusteeship. The court insisted that a trustee was compelled not to compete with the interests of investors and must give the bondholders undivided loyalty, free from any conflicting personal interest. The court compelled the trustee to pay over to the bondholders sums collected by the trustee on its loan to the borrower.

York v. *Guaranty Trust Co. of New York.*[36] The bondholders claimed that they had suffered loss by reason of the trustee's inaction. The trustee had enabled the borrower to meet payments of interest by making private loans to the borrower, but nevertheless the trustee failed to exercise its powers to commence liquidation proceedings and thereby to prevent further erosion of the assets. Subsequently the trustee proposed a scheme of arrangement involving the exchange of bonds for shares which was not accepted by all the bondholders. The court held that the trustee's motive for failing to liquidate was its desire to protect its position as a creditor, and that mere disclosure of the conflict could not exculpate the trustee. It was wilful misconduct and bad faith to occupy conflicting roles.

Dudley v. *Mealey.*[37] The defendant bank, which was a trustee under a bond issue, set off amounts owing to it privately against deposits held by it as a bank. The court insisted that the trustee should disgorge these sums received by set-off on the basis that the set-off had robbed the bondholders of an asset of the issuer. By becoming trustee the banker assumed a duty of undivided

---

35. 98 F. Supp. 807 (SDNY 1951), *rev'd* 201, F. 2d 635 (2d Cir. 1953) *modifying* 196 F. 2d 668 (2d Cir. 1952), *appeal dismissed*, 346 US 863 (1953).
36. 143 F. 2d 503 (2d Cir. 1944) *rev'd* on statute of limitations grounds 326 US 99 (1945).
37. 147 F. 2d 268 (2d Cir. 1945), *cert. denied* 325 US 873 (1945).

loyalty and was not free to enter into relations with the borrower which created a conflict of interest.

Other countries

In *Canada* the Canada Business Corporation Act prescribes by section 78 that if there is a material conflict of interest between the trustee's role as trustee and his role in any other capacity, then within 90 days after he becomes aware of the conflict the trustee must either eliminate the conflict or resign from office. This provision is based on a similar provision in the US Trust Indenture Act of 1939.[38]

The *Singapore* Companies Act[39] deems that the following offend the independence rule for regulated trusteeships of corporate public issues in Singapore: the trustee or a group company holds more than 5% of the voting power of the borrower's shares; the borrower owes money beneficially to the trustee or a group company, subject to a detailed threshold of 10% of the debentures (this effectively rules out bank trustees); the trustee has guaranteed the debentures.

The *Australian* Companies Code 1981[40] sets out independence tests on similar lines.

The *Luxembourg* 1972 Decree on trustees requires that *fiduciaire representants* (a special creation of a Luxembourg decree in the early 1970's to improve Luxembourg's acceptability to the capital markets) must be independent of the issuer and its controllers and must not find themselves in a position liable to create a conflict of interest. A non-complying trustee must rectify the position in three months or resign. No examples of conflict are given.

In *France* Decree-Law of 1935 for the Protection of Bondholders similarly proscribes certain conflicts of interest.

Contracting-out

The stringent rule that contracting-out is subject to the informed consent of the beneficiary supports specific disclosure in the prospectus. Thus if the trustee is also banker to the issuer, consideration should be given as to whether the full scale of the involvement should be disclosed if it is really significant. Further, even if the bondholder has consented, a conflict may expose the trustee to the risk of closer

38. Section 310.
39. Section 97.
40. Section 152.

scrutiny of the trustee's conduct and to allegations of bad faith destroying any exculpatory protection.

In *England*, contracting out of the conflicts rule for trustees is not in itself prohibited subject to the informed consent of the beneficiary, and subject to section 192 of the Companies Act 1985. English trust deeds contain exclusion clauses which purport to sanction certain conflicts of interest. These clauses do not sanction conflicts of interest generally: they merely, for example (a) allow cross-directorship, (b) allow the trustee or its officers to enter into other financial transactions with the obligor (including banking, insurance or underwriting contracts) or to deal in the bonds or other securities of the borrower, and (c) allow the trustee to act as trustee for another issue of the same borrower. Such clauses are necessary to enable a business trustee to act at all, because of the harsh prohibitions imposed on private trustees.

BANKING SECRECY AND THE ENFORCEMENT OF SECURITIES LEGISLATION

Lawrence Collins

INTRODUCTION

Confidentiality or secrecy is almost universally regarded as an essential ingredient in the relationship between customer and banker. But not all countries deal with the consequences of that ingredient in the same way. Some countries have a stronger policy than others to support it, and accordingly use their criminal law to protect secrecy, and make unlawful disclosure of bank secrets a criminal offence. This is so, in, for example, Switzerland, Luxembourg and the Cayman Islands. Other countries, such as England, Canada and the United States restrict the liability for breach of confidentiality to a civil remedy, and it is of course well-known that the English rule of banking confidentiality is relatively weak. The starting point for any discussion is the classic statement of Bankes LJ in *Tournier* v. *National Provincial and Union Bank of England*[1] of the exceptions to the basic rule of confidentiality. Three of these exceptions are of little comfort to the customer, namely (a) where disclosure is under compulsion by law; (b) where there is a duty to the public to disclose; and (c) where the interests of the bank require disclosure.

The object of this paper is to show how civil and criminal confidentiality rules operate in the international context, where there is a temptation for the guilty, as well as for the innocent, to take advantage of banking secrecy, and particularly so where they are engaged in infringement of securities and revenue legislation. It will consider three topical problems: the first is the impact of foreign secrecy law on British banks and British securities legislation; the second is the impact of British law on foreign banks in relation to foreign securities legislation; and the third is the problem of the impact of US securities legislation on foreign banks in London.

British securities law and foreign bank secrecy

Section 212 of the Companies Act 1985 (in common with its predecessor, section 74 of the Companies Act 1981) is designed primarily to allow a company to investigate build-ups in holdings in its shares,

1. [1924] 1 KB 461, 473 (CA).

but there seems no reason in principle why it could not be used for wider purposes, perhaps including the investigation of insider dealing. Section 212 provides:–

'(1) A public company may by notice in writing require a person whom the company knows or has reasonable cause to believe to be or, at any time during the 3 years immediately preceding the date on which the notice is issued, to have been interested in shares comprised in the company's relevant share capital –

(a) to confirm that fact or (as the case may be) to indicate whether or not it is the case, and

(b) where he holds or has during that time held an interest in shares so comprised, to give such further information as may be required. ....'

By section 216(1) 'where notice is served by a company under section 212 on a person who is or was interested in shares of the company and that person fails to give the company any information required by the notice within the time specified in it, the company may apply to the court for an order directing that the shares in question be subject to the restrictions of Part XV of this Act'. The relevant restrictions (section 454) prevent transfer of the shares, the exercise of voting rights, the issue of shares by way of bonus, the payment of sums due by way of dividend etc., and section 455 makes a person liable to a fine for contravention of the restrictions. The Companies Act defines interest widely, and it includes beneficial owners and those who hold on behalf of beneficial owners.

A company in an attempt to find who the beneficial owners are may seek to get the information from, initially, the registered owner. That may be an English bank or a foreign bank holding as nominee for a foreign customer. The foreign customer in turn may be a foreign bank holding for an individual or corporate customer. In *F.H. Lloyd Holdings plc*[2] the company was a listed public company which served notices under the predecessor of section 212 of the Companies Act 1985 requiring 12 nominee companies, three of which were based in Jersey and nine of which in England, to state whether or not they were interested in holdings of shares registered in their names and, if they were not the sole beneficial owners, to state the name and address and the nature of the interest of any other person interested in the shares. When the English companies complied with the notices, they named six Swiss banks, a German bank and a Luxembourg

2. [1985] B.C.L.C. 293.

bank, which were then themselves served with notices. All of them declined or failed to comply with the notices, and the company obtained an ex parte order of an interlocutory or provisional nature whereby the shares in question were to be subject to the restrictions imposed by the Companies Act pending the determination of its application for a final order directing that the shares be subject to the restrictions.

The decision in this case concerned a parcel of 150,000 shares in the company, which were registered in the name of Geneva Nominees Limited, an English company, which had replied to the notice by saying that it held shares for Trade Development Bank of Luxembourg 'for account client'. The company served notice on the Luxembourg bank, but the notice was not replied to. The Luxembourg bank refused to provide the information since, if it did so without the consent of its customer, it would be subject to sanctions under the criminal law of Luxembourg, and opposed the application for restrictions for the same reason. The primary argument of the bank was that the words 'any person' in the relevant sections did not include a foreign corporation which could not and did not carry on business in the United Kingdom and had no presence there of any kind. It was held that the Act did apply to foreign banks which did not carry on business in England. The company whose shares were in question was an English company, whose articles of association constituted a contract, governed by English law, between the company and its members in respect of their ordinary rights as members. The member was Geneva Nominees Limited, an English company, and the shares in the company, being transferable only upon a register kept in England, were property situated in England. Although the shares were held on trust for the Luxembourg bank, the trust property was situated in England and the trustee was resident here, and therefore the Luxembourg bank's beneficial interest was also situated in England. It did not make any difference that the foreigner was not the contracting party and the legal owner of the contractual rights and the shares, but only the equitable owner, particularly where the equitable interest was situated in England. The judge, Nourse, J. said[3]:–

'Why should a true foreigner, while able to enjoy all the benefits of holding shares in an English company, be intended to escape the burdens? ...... I think that this is legislation which gives our courts power to deal with foreigners who are not here as regards

3. At pp. 299–300.

these matters, being matters whch, according to all principles ought to be adjudicated on by our courts. You can either say that his English contractual and proprietary rights give the true foreigner a notional or constructive presence here or, as I think would be more correct, that they render his actual whereabouts immaterial.'

The judge went on to indicate that there might be grounds under which the court had a discretion whether or not to continue the restrictions. It is clear from the judgment that it will be difficult to persuade a judge to exercise a discretion against the restriction, once the recipient of a notice has failed to give the information. As the judge pointed out, the terms of the relevant section do not impose any limitation on the power to require the specified information. Although it was not the function of the court to affix a rubber stamp to every notice which is served, it was not necessary for the company to show that it had some real ground for believing that the person interested in the shares might be someone who was seeking to build up a substantial holding in it. The court would not make an order where the requirement to give the information was frivolous or vexatious and 'there could well be many other circumstances where the exercise of a discretionary power would, on general principles, be inapproriate'. Thus, it is clear that the mere fact that the foreign bank is subject to foreign banking secrecy laws (which would render it liable to penal sanctions if it gave the information without the consent of a customer) in itself will not prevent the English court from ordering the restrictions under the Companies Act 1985 for failure to give the information, but it might be a factor in the exercise of the discretion, taken together with other elements such as the small number of shares or other material suggesting that there was no bona fide reason for the company to have the information.

But where the legislation applies, foreign banking secrecy laws will not be allowed to override the law. In *Re Ashbourne Investments Ltd.*[4] (the Marc Rich case) Templeman J allowed restrictions on the transfer of shares to stand because otherwise it would allow 'the Swiss bank and the customer to continue to frustrate the investigations and flout our law'.

Foreign legislation and banking secrecy in England

The Marc Rich case[5] was in essence an investigation into tax fraud, but similar questions can equally arise in relation to securities law

4. [1978] 1 WLR 1346.
5. See *X A.G. and others* v *A Bank* [1983] 2 All ER 464.

infringements. In the Marc Rich case there was an investigation into the crude oil trading of an American company which was the wholly-owned subsidiary of a Swiss company. In proceedings brought in the United States by the Department of Justice subpoenas were served on the Swiss company and its American subsidiary, and subsequently on Citibank in New York. The documents covered by the subpoena served on Citibank in the United States were in fact kept at its London branch in its capacity as bankers to the Swiss company. The Swiss company brought proceedings in England against the London branch of Citibank to restrain if from disclosing confidential information held by it in its capacity as banker. As Leggatt J. put it, the bank found itself in a predicament because the subpoena in the United States was binding on it, and the subpoena required the documents in London to be produced to the United States court; but the bank through its London branch was subject to the duty of confidentiality under English law and disclosure of the documents to the grand jury in the United States would constitute or create a breach of that duty of confidentiality.

The point of the application in England was that, under US law, 'foreign governmental compulsion' may be a factor in quashing a subpoena or mitigating the consequences of non-compliance with a subpoena, and so it would be useful for Citibank to be able to point to the injunction in mitigation of its refusal to comply with the US subpoena. Relying on the English rules as to confidentiality an interlocutory injunction was granted restraining the bank from complying with the United States subpoena. The judge concluded[6]:-

> '... I find it hard to believe that the bank is in any danger of being held to be in contempt, since the adequacy of the excuse that it makes for non-production of the documents sought is now obvious indeed. Any sanction imposed now on the bank would look like pressure on this court, whereas ... it is for the New York court to relieve against the dilemma, in which it turns out to have placed its own national, by refraining from holding it in contempt if contempt proceedings are issued.'

The circumstances in that dispute were particularly helpful to Citibank, but the artificiality of the device is clear, and it cannot be assumed that the United States courts will always react favourably for foreign injunctions, which in effect prohibit compliance with US law. A customer could not obtain an English injunction preventing

6. At p. 480.

an English bank from complying with an English subpoena, and United States courts have not looked with favour on attempts to hide behind foreign secrecy laws. Thus in the case involving insider trading in *St. Joe Minerals Corporation*[7] the Securities and Exchange Commission made an application for an order requiring the defendant, a Swiss bank, to provide the SEC with information relating to the identities of the principals for whom it had purchased stock and stock options on American Stock Exchanges in a New York corporation, St Joe Minerals Corporation. The New York court held that it had jurisdiction to grant the order because the Swiss bank operated in New York through a subsidiary. The question on the merits was whether the bank could decline to give the information because of Swiss banking secrecy law. The relevant options had been traded through the Philadelphia Stock Exchange and the stock was traded on the New York Stock Exchange, immediately prior to the announcement of a cash offer by a subsidiary of Seagram for all the common stock of St Joe. The transaction resulted in an overnight profit of about US$2 million. The main object of the action by the SEC was to find out who had given the Swiss bank instructions to purchase options and shares. The court, applying established United States law, held that a foreign law prohibiting disclosure was not decisive, and the court had to balance the competing interests of United States law and the foreign law. The court held that the bank had deliberately courted legal impediments and could not be heard to assert its good faith after its expectation was realised. The bank had acted in bad faith, and made deliberate use of Swiss nondisclosure law to evade, in a commercial transaction for profit to it, the strictures of American securities law against insider trading. It had made use of the American securities market and profited thereby, and could not rely on Swiss non-disclosure law to shield the activity. The Swiss bank had deposited the proceeds of the transaction in an American bank in its own name, and profited from the activity, and undertook the transactions fully expecting to use foreign law to shield it from the reach of United States law. The court concluded[8]:-

'It would be a travesty of justice to permit a foreign company to invade American markets, violate American laws if they were indeed violated, withdraw profits and resist accountability for itself and its principals for the illegality by claiming their anonymity under foreign law.'

7. *SEC* v. *Banca della Svizzera Italiana* (1981) 92 F2d 111.
8. At p. 119.

United States securities law, evidence in England, and foreign banking secrecy

But there can be cases in which there is co-operation between the United Kingdom and the United States to prevent banking secrecy from being used to cloak fraud. In the *Santa Fe* case[9] the Securities and Exchange Commission brought civil proceedings in New York alleging that insider trading had taken place prior to the announcement of the takeover of Santa Fe by Kuwait Petroleum Corporation. For the purposes of the New York proceedings, the Securities and Exchange Commission required evidence which was situated in England, i.e. documents and testimony from employees of a Luxembourg bank with a branch in England. Under the Hague Convention for the taking of evidence abroad, to which both the United Kingdom and the United States are parties, a judge in the United States may request the English court to arrange for the evidence to be collected or taken in England, and pursuant to this procedure[10] the English court made an order requiring examination of witnesses who had been employed in London by a Luxembourg bank, International Resources and Finance Bank S.A., through whose London branch purchases of stock and options in Santa Fe had taken place. The employees sought to set aside the order requiring their examination on the ground, inter alia, that they were forbidden by Luxembourg law from revealing the identity of clients of the bank. In that case the relevant information related mainly to the operation of the London branch, and there was considerable doubt as to whether Luxembourg law did in fact forbid the disclosure of the information, but whether or not it did forbid it, it was held that there was no real or substantial risk of the applicants being charged with any criminal offence in Luxembourg. But Drake J accepted that there might be circumstances in which it would be against the public interest to order disclosure of confidential information, since there was:

'a public interest in maintaining the confidential relationship between banker and client, so that wherever a banker seeks to be excused from answering a question which would involve the breach of that confidentiality, it is proper ... for the court to consider such a request and to judge it in the context of the circumstances in which it is made. There is ... also clearly a public interest, and a very strong one, in not permitting the confidential

9. (1984) 23 Int. Legal Materials 511.
10. Evidence (Proceedings in Other Jurisdictions) Act 1975.

relationship between banker and client to be used as a cloak to conceal improper or fraudulent activities, evidence of which would otherwise be available to be used in legal proceedings, whether here or abroad.'

Conclusions

A few tentative conclusions may be suggested in this difficult and complex area:-

1. Most systems of law provide for banking secrecy. But some systems have a stronger policy than others against it. The reasons are sometimes historical, sometimes commercial, but where there is a strong policy of this kind, as in Switzerland or the Cayman Islands, a conflict is likely to arise with other systems of law.

2. Where the policy is somewhat weaker, as in England, the conflict is not likely to be so strong, but it can arise in a milder form, as in the Marc Rich case.

3. Where there is a conflict the banker is in a dilemma; he has to choose whether to obey the law of the place where the banking relationship is centred, or to obey the law of the place which is trying to force him to reveal banking secrets. Ultimately this type of conflict, as the litigation in the United States relating to the Bank of Nova Scotia show, is a political problem, which cannot easily be solved by bankers, lawyers, or courts.

INDEX

PEAT MARWICK
independence declaration by partners and members, 57
International Register of Prohibited Securities, 57
rules restricting investment by partners and members, 41, 56

PROPERTY
agent, held by, for principal, 20
agent, of,
  sale of, 17, 62
  separate, 19
agent, purchase by, of, 2, 17, 62
trustee, held by agent as, 20

RECEIVER
accountant as, 34, 55

RESIGNATION
trustee of bond issues, by, 76, 79

RESTRICTIVE TRADE PRACTICES COURT
reference of Rules of Stock Exchange to, 7

RULES
conduct of business, xvi, 68
  appropriation of bargains, 73
  best execution rule, xvi, 73
  churning, 72
  compliance officers to supervise, xvi
  compliance with, xx
  customer agreements, on, 73
  enforcement of, xx, 9
  excessive charging, against, 72
  good faith and fair dealing, general duty of, xx
  information to client, on, 73
  limitations of, 74
  priority of client, xvi, 73
  protection of clients, for, 6
  remuneration-related abuses, for, 72
  scalping, 71
  shingle theory, 71
  suitable for client, transaction to be, 72
Securities and Investments board, by, xvi, 9
SROs, by, xvi, xviii, 1, 6
  breach of, 66
Stock Exchange, of, 6
  changes in, 7
  Restrictive Trade Practices Court, reference to, of, 7
  trustees, on, 77
trustees, for business,
  England, in, 76, 80
  United States, in, 77